Level Up
Your Dog Training

How to Teach Your Dog Anything
(Some Assembly Required)

NATALIE BRIDGER WATSON, CPDT-KA

First published by Underfoot Publishing 2021

Copyright © 2021 by Natalie Bridger Watson

All rights reserved. No part of this publication may be reproduced, stored or transmitted in any form or by any means, electronic, mechanical, photocopying, recording, scanning, or otherwise without written permission from the publisher. It is illegal to copy this book, post it to a website, or distribute it by any other means without permission.

Natalie Bridger Watson has no responsibility for the persistence or accuracy of URLs for external or third-party Internet Websites referred to in this publication and does not guarantee that any content on such Websites is, or will remain, accurate or appropriate.

Designations used by companies to distinguish their products are often claimed as trademarks. All brand names and product names used in this book and on its cover are trade names, service marks, trademarks and registered trademarks of their respective owners. The publishers and the book are not associated with any product or vendor mentioned in this book. None of the companies referenced within the book have endorsed the book.

First edition

ISBN: 978-1-955179-01-0

Editing by Eileen Anderson

Contents

Acknowledgements   ix

How Dog Training Works

Introduction   3
    Why I Wrote This Book   3
    The Theory Dilemma   5
    Skills You Will Learn   6
    Think Positive   7
Choosing Reinforcers   9
    Reinforcement Drives Behavior   9
    Why Use Food?   11
    Toy Reinforcers   13
    Life Rewards   14
    Social Reinforcers   16
    Moralizing Reinforcement   17
    Dogs Don't Understand Debt   19
Using Food For Training   21
    Count Your Blessings: The Reinforcers You're
    Already Using   21
    The Ammunition Argument   22
    Becoming the Food Bowl   24
    The Rosy Glow of the Good Stuff   25
The Magic Marker   27
    What Is Clicker Training?   27

Why Do We Use a Clicker?	28
Can't I Just Say "Yes"?	30
Charging Your Marker	31
The Importance of Order	33
Marker Timing Drills	35
Why Timing Matters	35
Clicker Timing Exercises: Tennis Ball and TV	36
Why Delivery Matters	38
Food Delivery Exercises	39
Contextual Learners	42
Starting In Kindergarten	42
Boredom? I Don't Think So	43
When to Move On	46

Skill Building

Offered Versus Cued Attention	51
Hooray, Your First Training Exercise!	51
My Pet Peeve About "Watch Me"	52
Attention Is the Dog's Choice	54
Learning to See the Good	55
Hands Off, Mouth Closed	57
Trusting the Process	58
Targeting: Hand Target	61
What Is Targeting?	61
What Does a Hand Target Look Like?	62
How to Teach a Hand Target	62
Troubleshooting	63
When Will I Ever Use This?	65
Capturing: Default Sit	67
What Is Capturing?	67

Why Is Capturing Amazing?	68
Teaching Your Dog to Be Stubbornly Good	69
What Types of Behaviors to Capture	71
Building a Default Sit	72
Luring: Spin	**75**
What Is Luring?	75
Benefits of Luring	76
Downfalls of Luring	77
Luring a Spin in Both Directions	78
Luring a Down	81
Fading a Lure: Down	**83**
Fading a Lure Quickly and Smoothly	83
Lure to Hand Sign	85
Side Note: Why Hand Signs Rock	87
Shaping: Settle on a Mat	**88**
What Is Shaping?	88
Benefits of Shaping	89
Downfalls of Shaping	90
Easy Intro Shaping Games	91
Shaping Four Paws in a Box	93
Shaping Go to Mat	95
Shaping a Settle on the Mat	98
Attaching a Cue: Potty	**101**
Yay, You Finally Get to Talk!	101
How Cues Work	102
The Difference Between Cues and Commands	104
Attaching the Cue	106
Troubleshooting Cues	108

Self-Control Behaviors

Voluntary Leave It	115
The Skill That Will Save Your Dog's Life	115
Leave It = Turn Away + Eye Contact	116
Building Impulse Control with Slow Treats	117
Adding Eye Contact	119
Resisting Temptation	121
Installing the Zen Force Field	122
Attaching the Cue to Leave It	125
Very Important! How to NOT Break This Behavior	127
Building A Stay: Duration, Distraction, Distance	130
Raising the Bar	130
Boiling Frogs in Dog Training	131
Building Duration	133
Building Distraction	135
Building Distance	138
Oops! Troubleshooting Errors	140
Combining Criteria	141
Generalizing and Proofing	143
Generalists and Specialists	143
Generalizing to New Environments	144
Proofing Handler Positions	145
Cue Discrimination	146
Differential Reinforcement: Jumping Prevention	148
What Is Differential Reinforcement and Why Should You Care?	148
Teaching Four on the Floor	149

Leash Manners

Loose Leash Walking	157
Your Graduation Project	157
Why Most Dogs Pull	158
By Your Powers Combined	159
Captured Heel Position	160
Kindergarten: Indoors, Off Leash	160
Loose Leash Walking Equipment	161
What Goes in Which Hand	161
Lucky Lefts	163
Building Duration	166
Lured Turns	167
When You Might Need Tight Turns	167
Luring Right Turns	167
Luring Left Turns	169
Step Back Reset	171
Teaching a Yellow Light	171
Circle Method Reset	174
Red Light: When to Circle	174
What the Circle Method Looks Like	175

Dog Meet World

Leashes and Thresholds	181
Working with Distractions on Leash	181
"Tame" Distractions and "Wild" Distractions	182
Yo-Yo Leave It Practice	184
Management	187
An Ounce of Prevention is Worth a Pound of Cure	187
Are You in Trainer Mode? If Not, Then Manage	188
Environmental Cues	190
What Are Environmental Cues?	190
Sit at Doorways	192
Sit for the Leash	194
Voicemail Behavior	194
Fading Reinforcement	197
Moving to Life Rewards	197
Behavioral Bank Accounts and Canine Credit Scores	201
But Wait, We Never Taught Him "NO!"	203
In Conclusion	206
Solving the Theory Dilemma	206
About the Author	208
Bonus Lectures	209
Mental Versus Physical Exercise	209
Moving Beyond the Bowl	210
Kong as Babysitter	211
Ring a Bell to Go Outside	213
Why We Don't Say Hi on Leash	215
No, You Can't Pet My Dog	217
Trail and Sidewalk Manners	218
In Case of Emergency: It's Okay to Lure Past	220

Acknowledgements

For Coda, who made dog training look effortless.
For Haven, who *emphatically* didn't.

And for Eileen, who does not give herself enough credit.

1

How Dog Training Works

Introduction

Why I Wrote This Book

With pages of dog training information a few clicks away on the internet, why do we need another dog training book to reinvent the wheel?

The difference is that most of the dog training books fall into one of two categories. I think of them as "give a man a fish" books and "teach a man to fish" books.

"Give a man a fish" books are geared toward the general public. They're very approachable, recipe-based training guides without a lot of jargon or theory. These books are the "just tell me what to do and we'll worry about why later" kind of books.

And on the opposite end of the spectrum are the "teach a man to fish" books, which are written by and for dog trainers. These books assume that you want to do a lot of this dog training stuff and will be reading a small library's worth of additional training books to round out your education.

And in the middle of those categories is a gap that I hope this book will fill.

I've written *Level Up Your Dog Training* for dog lovers who want to learn how to train their pets, but who also want to know *why* to do those things.

The ideal reader of this book wants the training recipe to solve their problem in the short term, but they also want to know the basics of how and why it works so they can make their own recipes in time—without having to become a dog trainer to do it!

My goal with this book is to combine a beginner-level obedience class curriculum with a broad-but-shallow understanding of the theory behind what we're doing. By the end of this book, you should have the tools to improvise as needed.

Will it make you a professional dog trainer?

Heck no.

Will it give you a deeper understanding than a face-value recipe with no explanation for *why* you're doing what you're doing?

I hope so.

And for those aspiring dog trainers who stumble upon this book, I hope that it will make an approachable entry point into the field—a launching pad toward bigger and better things.

This book assumes that you have a dog to work with and that you want help with pet obedience and day-to-day life manners. It also assumes that you are curious and willing to have a little fun in the process.

By the end of this book, if you work through all the training exercises as prescribed, I hope that you will have two things:

First, a better behaved dog.

And second, a general understanding of how that happened, including how to use those same skills to improve other aspects of your life with your dog beyond the scope of this book.

You can have a well-behaved dog without taking them to task, scolding them or pushing them around—and you can get results much faster than you ever dreamed.

INTRODUCTION

The Theory Dilemma

I started teaching basic obedience classes about a decade before writing this book.

In that time, I've wrestled with a dilemma that I've never solved to my own satisfaction.

I call it the Theory Dilemma. In a nutshell: Trying to find the balance between long-term theory and short-term practice within a short one-hour window is an exercise in frustration.

My clients always want practical, hands-on exercises to train their dogs immediately. That's why they hired me! They want to be able to see big progress within a one-hour lesson. All practice and no theory sounds *great* to them.

But as a professional, I know that they would benefit tremendously from understanding the theory so they could apply the same skill in other situations down the line without having to hire me every time they need to teach a new behavior. Because the training skills you learn in the average puppy class *are* transferable and replicable—*if* you have enough theory to understand how to apply them to new problems.

There just wasn't enough time in class to get all the relevant information into my clients' heads, no matter how hard both parties were trying. My lessons became a sort of triage—just enough theory to hold up this behavior, but never quite enough for them to apply the same principle to the next behavior. I always wanted to be able to give my clients a little bit more support on the theory side *without* taking away any of their practice time.

This book is my compromise and my attempt to solve the Theory Dilemma.

It's also the handbook included with all my obedience classes, which allows me to trust that my students have access to the theory if they want it. That way they can focus on the practical applications within their lesson times and I can sleep better at night knowing that the theory is available to them when they're ready for it.

This book will show you the training tools you already have and how you can apply them in the future.

I firmly believe in the power of citizen scientists. I want to empower my students and clients to tackle training problems on their own years after they've worked with me. I want to give them enough information that they never need to hire me again because they can troubleshoot their dog's behavior on their own in the future.

I hope that this book gives you similar tools!

Skills You Will Learn

By the end of this book, your dog will know how to sit, lie down, go to a mat, stay, come when called, leave things alone, spin in a circle, walk politely on a loose leash, give you their attention, potty quickly when asked, wait at doorways, sit for their leash, stand calmly for petting instead of jumping, and tell you where they'd prefer to be petted.

That sounds like a pretty well-behaved dog, right?

Even more exciting are the skills that *you* will learn while teaching those things!

While working through the exercises in this book, you will learn how to use a clicker to train your dog to do basic obedience skills. Layered in at the same time, you'll pick up general principles that you can apply to whatever training goals come up over the course of your dog's life.

You will learn how to use a marker signal to change behavior without having to push your dog around or "show them who's boss."

You'll learn the four critical building blocks for all sorts of different behaviors: luring, targeting, capturing and shaping, and when to use each one.

You'll learn how to mix-and-match those methods to come up with the best solution to problem behaviors in the future, and you'll apply all four of them together to teach your dog truly beautiful leash manners as your graduation project.

This book is every bit as much about training people as it is about training dogs. I hope you take this information and run with it.

At the end of the book, if you have a well-trained dog but no idea how you got there or how to handle the next behavior outside of the context of this book, then I haven't done my job. I want you to leave feeling like you have the skills to accomplish whatever you set your mind to.

And if working your way through this book means you don't need to hire me as a trainer after all because you can solve your dog's problems on your own, then that means I've done my job. My job as a writer is to educate you so well that I put myself out of business as a trainer.

I hope you are as eager to learn as I am to teach you!

Think Positive

In the past few decades, dog training has undergone a quiet but profound revolution.

Years ago, we believed that dog training was a matter of "do it or else." The humans gave commands and the dogs obeyed. If the dogs didn't obey, the humans "corrected" the dog by making them uncomfortable in various ways, either physically or emotionally, so the dogs would understand that they had erred. If you trained your dog when you were growing up, this is probably the model you're familiar with.

You've likely heard that a training class taught with positive reinforcement is desirable. But what does that mean in a practical sense and why is that something to look for when you are hiring a trainer?

Positive reinforcement is what happens when a behavior is increased (**reinforced**) by the addition (**positive**) of something that the dog wants.

Or in other words, it's building behaviors by strategically giving dogs rewards instead of waiting for the dog to get it wrong and punishing them for it, which was the previous model.

There are dozens of reasons why we prefer to train without the use of **aversives** (threatening or uncomfortable things, things the dog works to avoid), but the gist of it is that they're unnecessary and often carry the risk of negative side effects later in the training process, even the methods that seem relatively harmless in the moment.

We're going to focus on systematically building the good behaviors we want to see instead of punishing the behaviors we don't.

At its most basic, the sequence of training that we're going to follow is: Cue -> Behavior -> Click -> Treat. In other words, we are going to ask for a response from the dog (**cue**), the dog is going to do something in response to that request (**behavior**), we are going to use a clicker to mark that this behavior was correct (**click**), and we are going to pay them for their effort (**treat**).

While simple, this methodology is robust and builds long-lasting behaviors that can hold up under the pressures of real life: no "or else" necessary.

Choosing Reinforcers

Reinforcement Drives Behavior

Behavior is almost infinitely complex. Cats lick their coats to clean themselves, raccoons wash their food, monkeys throw poop, humans read books and dogs bury their bones in the back garden for later. Despite the wide range of behaviors we see in the world, the driving factors behind these behaviors are shockingly simple.

At the end of the day, it's all about The Good Stuff and The Bad Stuff.

Behavior doesn't happen in a vacuum—which is to say, the point of behavior is to achieve some sort of consequence.

If you're thirsty and you get something to drink, the behavior of pouring a glass of lemonade will lead to the consequence of decreasing your thirst.

If you woke up this morning and went to work, that behavior will be reinforced with a paycheck and the continued ability to pay your bills.

And so on.

These consequences can be broadly separated into four categories:

1. Adding more of The Good Stuff to increase behavior (**positive reinforcement**)

2. Removing some of The Good Stuff to decrease behavior (**negative punishment**)

3. Removing some of The Bad Stuff to increase behavior (**negative reinforcement**)

4. Adding more of The Bad Stuff to decrease behavior (**positive punishment**)

In these cases, "positive" and "negative" can be thought of in their mathematical sense as "additive" and "subtractive" rather than in their moralized sense as "good" and "bad."

You have probably heard that positive reinforcement is the best place to begin when training a dog, but if you're like most of my clients, you may be a bit fuzzy on what that specifically means if asked. It's a lot more specific than just "being nice to dogs" or "setting fair boundaries," which are the answers I get most often.

Positive reinforcement means that you are becoming a source of The Good Stuff: food, toys, petting, praise, access to walks, access to novelty, access to other dogs, or anything else your dog will happily work to earn.

Things which are not positive reinforcement include: fussing, scolding, intimidating, clapping your hands, spraying with water, shaking noisy things, throwing startling things, alpha rolling, shocking, stimming, vibrating, beeping, pinching, choking, correcting, or the ever-present "TSST." Those are techniques that involve teaching your dog to avoid The Bad Stuff. As a rule of thumb, if it comes after the behavior and means "stop that," it's not positive reinforcement.

For the purposes of this book, we're not going to spend much time talking about The Bad Stuff—because really, who wants to be sharp with their dog if they don't have to?

Instead, we're going to work to leverage The Good Stuff to build robust behaviors without compromising our dogs' emotional health or damaging our relationship with them. Being kind doesn't make you a pushover and it doesn't mean that your dog gets to run roughshod through the house.

If you read the list above and felt a guilty twinge because the things on The Bad Stuff list sound a bit familiar, you're not alone. You'll learn viable alternatives here so you don't feel the need to rely on those options in the future. The better you get at working with The Good Stuff, the less often you'll feel tempted to bring out The Bad Stuff.

Why Use Food?

Most of the time, when we're talking about using The Good Stuff for training, we're talking about food.

Why?

We need some sort of motivator that our dogs are very interested in earning. In order to use The Good Stuff to build behavior with positive reinforcement, it's pretty important that the learner actually wants to obtain the reward we're going to leverage. Food is an effective currency for everything with a pulse—if we didn't behave to obtain food, we would all starve to death shortly after birth.

Using a currency that your learner values is critical to training success.

For example, if you went to work and your boss decided to pay you in expired coupons instead of dollars and cents, I'm going to hazard a guess that you probably would not stay employed at that job for very long. Fundamentally, expired coupons and dollar bills are both pieces of paper with some representative text printed on them that we've collectively decided have some sort of value. But regardless of your boss's intentions, that attempted reinforcer would not be motivating enough for you to continue behaving, i.e., working.

Likewise, the value of our dog's effort is going to match the value of their "paycheck," and for most dogs, that means that food is going to be one of their big-ticket reinforcers.

Food is quick to consume, easy to dispense, easily carryable in a pocket or pouch, and most dogs will work for a lot of it before getting bored (or full). You can work with food for an extended period of time and still have a dog who wants what you've got. It's incredibly convenient compared to a non-food reinforcer such as a walk, for example—which is also a very effective motivator, but not something you can realistically deploy at the drop of a hat dozens of times a day contingent on your dog's behavior unless you're in much better shape than I am.

Food also allows us to use a sort of sliding scale for effort. The value of the reinforcer should match the amount of effort that the dog put in to achieve it. Sitting for three seconds in the middle of the kitchen is a kibble sort of skill. Doing six backflips in a row in the middle of a crowded auditorium? That's steak territory.

There's an unfortunate cultural stigma against using food in training—especially, heaven forbid, "people food." Some people mistakenly believe that using food will create a dog who begs at the table, a dog who only listens when you wave a cookie in front of his nose first, or an obese dog.

Fortunately, these are all issues of user error rather than inherent problems with food. I've been training professionally for a decade at this point and I can assure you that my dogs do not beg at the table, they listen just fine and I keep them at appropriate weights without difficulty.

In Ye Olde Days when dog training was traditionally compulsion-based, there were a lot of myths about how training with food was "bribery," how it would "reduce your status" and how your dog would become unreliable unless you "showed them the money" first.

Bluntly: This is unscientific fear-mongering.

As a certified professional dog trainer, I'm here to give you official permission to use food to train your dog.

In fact, I am going to *insist* that you do. For the purposes of this book, using food in training is not optional: it's mandatory.

We're going to talk about this in more detail shortly, but let's talk about a few more options you have for leveraging The Good Stuff in your training. While food will be our primary tool, you can and should supplement it with non-food reinforcers as well (in *addition to*—not as a substitution for—food).

Toy Reinforcers

If your pup knows how to play tug, fetch or play with dog toys, you have a few more options for The Good Stuff when training your dog.

Play is an incredibly effective reinforcer for many dogs, especially for dogs who tend to be more active such as terriers, retrievers and herding breeds. If your dog isn't really that into toys but they love to play wrestling, "bitey face" or chase-me games, those are perfectly valid options for building behavior too. But they tend to be less convenient than food for a couple of reasons.

First, they just take longer. I can absolutely guarantee that my dog can swallow a piece of cheese much faster than your dog can retrieve a ball. Since training involves repetition, that means I'm going to get in a lot more reps training with food in the same amount of time.

Second, toys tend to require some amount of space. It takes almost no space whatsoever for me to dispense a piece of food into my German Shepherd's mouth, and quite a bit more room for me to throw a frisbee for her. Where we deliver the reinforcer is also going to affect the final behavior and I can be a lot more precise with a piece of food the size of a pea than a toy I have to chuck across a yard.

And third, the type of reinforcer we use is going to affect the emotional flavor of the behavior. I know that sounds a bit "woo woo" mystical, but stick with me. The emotional association with the reinforcer is going to get sort of glommed onto the behavior itself. Since the dogs who are motivated by toys tend to have very high emotions around them ("OH BOY, OH BOY, THROW IT!"), that intense energy tends to bleed over onto the behavior itself.

So for example, all other things being equal, a down-stay taught with food (even with a very food-motivated dog) tends to be more thoughtful and a down-stay taught with a toy tends to be more alert... which is not necessarily a good thing if you just wanted to have lunch on a pet-friendly patio and your dog is quivering with enthusiasm and ready to launch up at a moment's notice.

For the most part, I prefer to use toys to maintain behaviors that I've already taught. I use food to train the behavior initially and then start adding in other types of reinforcers once the behavior is at a skill level I'm happy with.

Life Rewards

Life rewards are a powerhouse of reinforcement hiding in plain sight. In fact, you're probably already using them without even knowing it!

Life rewards are all of the other pleasant things in your dog's day that you contribute to, such as going outside for a walk, chewing on chew toys, going out to the yard, playing with ice cubes, being brushed (if your dog enjoys grooming), being invited onto the sofa or bed, greeting people, playing with other dogs, and anything else that makes a dog's life enjoyable.

Of course, some of these are easier to deploy strategically than others. If I were trying to build a new behavior by reinforcing it exclusively with exercise walks, the number of practice reps I could get through in a day would be limited by my cardiovascular health and the distance my legs can walk (much to my poor dogs' dismay). It would take *ages* for me to get a substantial number of repetitions in if I could only use that reinforcer a couple of times a day.

Does that mean that we write off life rewards as impractical? Absolutely not! But it does mean being thoughtful about when we use them.

You can and should use these strategically to reinforce behaviors that you like when they happen. A broad variety of life rewards will increase your dog's quality of life immensely. But as with toys, life rewards are probably not the most practical place to start when it comes to building new behaviors from scratch. Life rewards tend to be more effective for maintaining known behaviors that you've built in other ways.

In other words, feel free to use as many life rewards to reinforce good behavior as possible because you can definitely benefit from that— but don't try to use life rewards as your *exclusive* reinforcement. You'll get there faster if you use food and you don't get bonus points for being inefficient.

It's also worth noting that life rewards are very often the driving force behind the naughty behaviors that test your patience with your pup.

For example, let's say you pull out your dog's leash and they start going bonkers: tap-dancing feet, racing to the door, barking and whining, leaping into the air, the whole canine rodeo. If you clip the leash on them and take them for a walk after they've gone into joyful hysterics, you have reinforced *all* of that hyperactive behavior, whether you meant to or not. (I'm gonna go out on a limb and assume you probably didn't mean to, unless you enjoy being gleefully trampled.) And the more often that exuberant behavior leads to a walk, the stronger that habit will become.

Likewise, if making puppy-dog eyes at the dinner table reliably scores scraps, you're going to build a dog who begs. If your dog learns that leaping on the guests makes the guests look at them, talk to them, touch them, engage with them and sometimes even play with them "to calm them down," you'll have a canine kangaroo bouncing three feet in the air every time the door opens in no time.

When I'm trying to decrease a behavior I don't like, one of the first things I check is whether there's a life reward currently paying my dog for that behavior. It's often much easier to just rearrange that life reward so it occurs after a behavior I want to see *more* of, and make sure that it *never* happens after the behavior that I want to see *less* of. This sort of lifestyle fine-tuning can make a remarkable difference in your dog's overall behavior.

PS: Don't sweat it if you give your dog nice things for free too. Being kind to your dog is not a sin or a sign of weakness and the existence of life rewards does *not* imply that all good things in life must be earned. In case you need it, I hereby give you Official Dog Trainer Permission to be nice to your dog for free too.

Social Reinforcers

"But wait!" I can hear you say, "What about petting, praise and telling her she's a good dog?"

Yes, we'll be using plenty of social reinforcement along the way. Assuming your dog likes it (which not all dogs do), you're welcome to pet and praise to your heart's content. Physical touch and kind words are both excellent ways to build your bond with your dog, especially when they're used in conjunction with other reinforcers.

However.

Most dogs enjoy social reinforcers when there's not much else on offer. It tends to be one of the weaker reinforcers for building strong obedience behaviors over time.

In terms of human paychecks, petting and praise are the equivalent of a lovely thank-you card and a hug. If my friend asked me to do something once in a while that was really no trouble at all and they paid me with a lovely thank-you card and a hug, I would feel pretty good about that interaction. But if my boss tried to give me a hug-salary and write my paycheck in thank-you cards, I would need to have a conversation with human resources and I would be updating my resume ASAP.

Social reinforcers are like a condiment or a spice. They make other reinforcers more special, but they're not terribly "filling" as a stand-alone meal. Trying to train your dog entirely using praise and petting is like trying to meet your caloric needs entirely with ketchup. Can you do it? Umm, probably. Would you want to? Probably not.

And as a side note: a trainer who claims that their major form of positive reinforcement is petting and praise is not demonstrating advanced skill or "good energy." On the contrary: it's a gigantic red flag that they missed the bus on the dog training revolution we talked about in the last chapter. In the vast majority of cases, it means that there is a heavy dose of "or else" in their training and all of that lovely-sounding petting and praise is backed up by intimidation, threat or physical correction, which just wipes the rose-colored film right off that image.

As mentioned, this is not a book about leveraging The Bad Stuff, which means that there's no shame in my game when it comes to making liberal use of The Good Stuff. I'm happy to add some social-reinforcer ketchup to my options as a garnish, but I'm not going to pretend it's a balanced diet on its own. You shouldn't either.

Moralizing Reinforcement

You may have noticed a theme in the previous sections to the tune of, "Yes, this reinforcer is nice too and I acknowledge that it is an option, but at the end of the day, we're mostly going to be using food."

This makes some people feel uncomfortable at first and I want to take a moment to talk about it, because I think it's hugely important.

I've met some truly incredible trainers in my life. I'm talking world-class people training service dogs, bomb sniffing dogs, obedience-championship-winning dogs, dogs in movies, freaking *wild elephants* and military-trained *spy-cats (YES,* that was a real thing! they trained actual cats! as spies! for the military!), and *every single one of them uses food to train.*

One hundred percent.

But outside of professional training circles, there is a weird sort of moralizing that gets attached to reinforcement strategies. Pet owners are often quick to assure me that their dog is trained *"without* treats," as if I wouldn't take their accomplishments seriously if they'd actually *paid* the dog.

I can't count the number of times a random stranger has seen my service dog being her amazing self out in public, complimented her training with borderline reverence and then noticed the treat bag on my hip.

"Oh," they say, deflating or with scorn, as if that somehow discredits my dog's behavior. "No wonder she's being so good; you have *treats."*

Well, yes?

Also, that's her dinner, but that's beside the point.

If you're acknowledging that the mere presence of treats is all it takes to get excellent behavior (and oh how I wish the bar was that low), why in the world would you choose not to use them? That's just cutting off your nose to spite your face!

In short: There's nothing inherently more virtuous about using less valuable reinforcers to train a behavior. If someone assures me that they trained their dog without treats, that does not make me respect them—it makes me think, "Well, that was probably really inefficient. I hope you weren't in a hurry."

Your dog's behavior is sculpted by its consequences. You can train with The Good Stuff or you can train with The Bad Stuff, but you don't get to opt out. If it has an effect on your dog's long-term behavior, it goes in one of those buckets. And if I have to choose between treats and threats, I'm choosing treats.

I choose to use The Good Stuff bucket as much as humanly possible. The things in The Good Stuff bucket are powerful, they're kind and they improve my relationship with my dog because they make me the source of The Good Stuff. The things in The Bad Stuff bucket may also be powerful in some cases, but they come with risks that I'd rather not mess with, such as being correlated with higher levels of avoidance, slower behavior, aggression and deteriorating the relationship between dog and owner.

And the most efficient thing in The Good Stuff bucket, the gold-standard of dog training, is using food.

Dogs Don't Understand Debt

Once in a while, I'll get this comment, so I wanted to go ahead and address it here.

"But I feed my dog, I walk him, I play with him, I pay for the roof over his head, I do *everything* for him. Shouldn't he just [fill in the blank] because he loves me?"

While that is a beautiful sentiment, it doesn't go very far in animal training.

Dogs are wonderful creatures, but they have no concept of debts, gratitude or mortgages. They may love your company and adore every minute that they spend with you, but at the end of the day, "pleasing you" is still not a primary reinforcer for your dog and treating it like the holy grail of dog training is doing yourself a huge disservice.

If your dog had to choose between a piece of cheese and pleasing you (and, critically, if pleasing you had never been backed up by the threat of scolding or various flavors of The Bad Stuff if you were *dis*pleased), your dog would choose the cheese ten times out of ten.

He just would.

My dogs absolutely do want to make me happy (because, as mentioned, I have two thumbs and access to all of The Good Stuff). They want to make me happy because it works out very well for them. But they want to make me happy *because* my happiness reliably comes with benefits, such as cheese.

If you've ever worked for someone who didn't appreciate your efforts or who consistently paid too little and too late, you know what that feels like. I'm not talking about the tough-love leader who held you to high standards but ultimately played fair—I'm talking about the one who asked you to put in a bunch of effort and *never* made it worth your while.

How did you feel about going to work/school with that boss/teacher? Did you give them your best effort? Did you feel good about your contributions? Did you go home at the end of the day feeling fulfilled? Probably not, because working hard for minimal reward is soul-crushing.

And on the flip side, if you've ever worked for a boss who recognized hard work and gave generous bonuses when they were merited, you know how motivating it can be to work with a leader who sees your potential and rewards effort at just the right level. A boss who gives bonuses, raises and incentives fairly based on performance is a lot more motivating to work for than a boss who threatens docked pay if they're displeased and expects their happiness to be its own reward for their employees.

Be a good boss.

Using Food For Training

Count Your Blessings: The Reinforcers You're Already Using

Since we've decided that we're going to be training primarily with The Good Stuff, it's helpful to take a moment to list out what that looks like for your dog.

We're going to be using a lot of food, but there are plenty of other things in The Good Stuff bucket, so let's inventory what we've got.

For most dogs, your Good Stuff list is going to start off something like this:

Food
Treats
Walks
Petting
Toys and play
Social play with people
Social play with dogs
Greeting people
Smelling new and exciting things
Seeing new and exciting things
Tasting new and exciting things
Going for car rides

Going swimming
And so on

But we can get even more granular than that, of course—types of food, car rides to different locations, greetings with strangers versus friends, a pecking order of toys, balls and tugs.

Go ahead! The more specific you can be with this list, the more options you'll have when it comes time to write paychecks for your dog.

While you're making the list, make a note to the side of each item of how your dog would rank it on a ten point scale, with a one being "Oh, neat, thanks I guess" and a ten being "OH MY GOD, TICKETS TO DISNEYLAND!!!" If they don't think in caps lock with multiple exclamation marks, it's not a ten. Try to think of a variety of things across the whole spectrum of wonderfulness. That way, we can match the paycheck to the effort required.

The Ammunition Argument

While we're talking about food, I am going to go out on a limb here and assume that you do not intend to starve your dog to death.

Bold claim, I know, but I'm comfortable gambling on it.

Feeding your dog their regular daily portion was part of what you signed up for when you brought home a dog. You probably planned for that by buying a food dish which you intended to fill somewhere between one and three times a day, every day, for the life of your dog.

If you're like a lot of my clients, you ask your dog to sit and wait while you put down the food bowl. Most people who hire me have trained a sit in their living room and their dog can successfully wait for the food bowl to hit the ground before eating—I can generally take that for granted.

First: Congratulations! You've successfully built a sturdy behavior with positive reinforcement by leveraging The Good Stuff!

But now we're going to take it to the next level.

To maintain a healthy weight, your dog is going to take in a certain number of calories per day in food, treats and chews, and they're going to burn a certain number of calories in activity (on top of their basal metabolic rate just to keep their kidneys doing kidney things and their lungs doing lung things, etc.).

That amount is going to vary dramatically between dogs, from a quarter of a cup a day for a toy-sized dog like a chihuahua to upward of six cups a day for a growing giant breed like a great dane.

But no matter how big their portion, I can pretty much bet that the majority of those calories for the chihuahua and for the great dane are going to be divided into one, two or three feedings, which means that you are going to be leveraging *all* of those calories per day on a maximum of three sit-stays.

Hmm.

That doesn't sound like a very good deal to me.

So here's what I'm suggesting instead. You're going to feed your dog every day no matter how good or naughty they are, because you love your dog and you want them to stay healthy.

But you can be strategic about it.

If you're going to give them, say, two cups of food per day, there is absolutely no reason that it needs to be one bowl in the morning and one bowl at night—and there are plenty of reasons why it shouldn't be, not least of which is that you're wasting an awful lot of your behavioral ammo.

So, a proposition: what if you could take the food that you're already going to give your dog for free anyway and use that to buy better behavior?

If your dog gets two meals a day, take your dog's morning meal and put it into a training pouch at the beginning of the day. Wear that while you're around the house with your dog. That's your "checkbook" for the morning so you can pay for good behavior when you see it. Don't feel like you need to dole out every kibble individually (because that can be a lot of training with a large-breed dog), but there are *plenty* of size units in between a full meal and a single piece of kibble.

At the end of the morning or when you're leaving for work, give your dog however much food you didn't use in training. They're still getting the same amount of food they would eat in their normal breakfast, but now you're using as much of it as you need for training and the freebies are the leftovers, not the whole thing.

In the evening when you get home, put your dog's dinner into your treat pouch and do the same thing. At the end of the night, the dog gets whatever is leftover in the pouch.

Don't throw away your ammunition.

Becoming the Food Bowl

Dogs, bless them, often have a very low bar for what counts as food.

Dry kibble? Food.

Biscuit treats? Food.

Dead frogs? Probably food.

But to build strong behaviors, we need strong reinforcers, and that means we want our dogs to be very interested in The Good Stuff we've got. Building your dog's enthusiasm for food will pay off in the long run.

During the training process, you're going to become your dog's food bowl. Put the metal, plastic or ceramic bowl away for the next several weeks—and as far as I'm concerned, feel free to donate it for good, but I understand if that's more of a commitment than you're willing to make a few pages into a book.

Think about it. How excited does your dog get when you pour his dinner? Pretty excited, I bet.

And don't you wish you could harness that enthusiasm to build good behavior all day long instead of using the whole thing on one maybe-thirty-second-but-probably-less sit stay?

You can! By becoming the new food bowl.

When I'm asking you to hand-feed your dog, I don't mean sticking your hand into a dog food bowl and making the dog eat around it. (And incidentally, that is more likely to *cause* resource guarding than to prevent or treat it.) What I mean is taking some amount of food, maybe a few pieces or maybe a handful depending on the situation, and either feeding it directly to your dog's mouth or delivering it to the floor for them to eat when they've done something you like. This has nothing whatsoever to do with resource guarding, status reduction or "dominance." It's not mystical; it's just an effective way to reinforce behavior.

The Rosy Glow of the Good Stuff

We've talked about how using food in training will benefit your dog's manners in terms of their obedience, but it's equally important to talk about how it will benefit your relationship with your dog.

At the risk of stating the obvious, if you use rewards to train your dog, you become their number one source of The Good Stuff, which means you're very relevant to their interactions with the world.

You don't have to play bad-cop or the strict parent who always ends the fun anymore. Your primary interaction with your dog can be facilitating a bunch of the stuff they love, which gives your dog a much stronger incentive to actually listen to you—after all, you're the golden ticket to everything wonderful in their world!

In contrast, for an untrained dog, their owners are usually the fun-police who remove the most interesting parts of their day. Most of the really Good Stuff an untrained dog encounters is by accident or off-limits. The wonderful stuff in their life is provided by the world at large and their loving owners are generally the people running after them yelling, "Stop digging! Don't greet that person! Walk slower! Don't sniff that! Dear god, *what's in your MOUTH!*"

Nobody wants to be that guy.

And you know what's even worse? The dogs with those well-meaning owners are very efficiently trained to ignore what their owners say. They learn how to steal food more sneakily, how to dodge grabbing hands faster and take advantage of lapses in attention to finally engage with some of The Good Stuff out in their world—because their owner has become the obstacle to work around, not the key ingredient to the fun. What a bummer!

When you train with the Good Stuff, not only does your dog get more Good Stuff in their life overall, but *you* become the star of the show. And just like the untrained dog starts looking for opportunities to engage with their environment (the main source of their Good Stuff), *your* dog will start to look to you for ideas about what behaviors are the most likely to pay off.

The Magic Marker

What Is Clicker Training?

To aid in our training adventure, we're going to use a small mechanical device called a clicker.

A clicker is exactly what it sounds like: it's a box that makes a click sound when you press it. It has no meaning to the dog outside of what you condition into it, so this is a "some assembly required" dog training tool.

A clicker allows us to tell the dog when they've done something right and earned a reward. The sequence will be: cue, behavior, click, treat. With repetition, the sound will become a predictor that the treat is coming.

The clicker is the way we attach the consequence (a treat) to the behavior (sitting, for example). It's sort of like glue that holds the behavior and its consequence together. It allows us to tell the dog specifically which part of the behavior we liked enough to put a treat on it, which tells them which behavior to repeat next time.

It's possible to "clicker train" without using a physical clicker (for example, my deaf dog who can't hear a clicker is still "clicker trained" with a thumbs-up marker), but a clicker is typically the most convenient option and the economy model only costs about a dollar at the pet store.

Buy a couple if you can—they're small and like many small objects, they tend to go missing eventually.

Once you've got your clicker, when your dog isn't in the room, go ahead and click it a few dozen times. Let your kids do the same if they'll be involved in training. Get it out of your system before it means anything to your dog—and bless you for your enthusiasm!

At this point, you'll also want to buy a treat pouch to hold your dog's paychecks if you haven't already. I prefer the Rapid Rewards bag made by The Clicker Company (previously Doggone Good) because it's the most durable one on the market in a decent price range, but any large sized washable treat bag should suffice. Terry Ryan, Outward Hound, Starmark and Hurtta make nice ones as well, although I prefer the Rapid Rewards' magnetic closure to the hinge-styles in this list.

The cylindrical drawstring models will work, but if you can spring for one of the better ones listed above, do.

Some cost-conscious clients have also repurposed nail aprons from home improvement stores or chalk bags from rock climbing. Anything easily washable that will hold about a cup of food will do (although I advise against actual pants pockets unless you enjoy finding dog food in the laundry on a regular basis).

Why Do We Use a Clicker?

A clicker allows us to pinpoint the exact moment the dog got the behavior right. It essentially buys us time between the correct behavior occurring and the reward appearing. That's why sometimes we call it a **"marker"** or a **"bridge"**—as in it marks the correct behavior and it bridges the gap between the behavior and the consequence.

For the purposes of this book, the words clicker, marker and bridge are interchangeable.

In practical terms, we use it because it speeds up your training and it means doing fewer repetitions to get the same results.

For example, if you have a very fast, very eager dog and you are trying to teach them how to sit, but they sit-down-roll-over-play-dead as one fast lump of behavior, a clicker is the behavioral scalpel you can use to tease apart those behaviors and explain to the dog that the *sit* part was what earned them this reward and the rest of it was unnecessary.

If you have a less fast, less eager dog, using a clicker to mean "food is coming" still gives you increased clarity.

It's worth adding that you won't be married to your clicker forever and yes, your dog will still obey you without it. It's a convenience, not an absolute necessity, but you'll want to give it a try.

We use a clicker during the teaching phase when the dog is still learning the parameters of the behavior, and also any time when we're going to stretch the behavior by teaching them how to do it in a harder situation than they've tried before. For example, we'd use a clicker to teach the initial skill to sit, then stop using it once the behavior was solid in that environment. But if we wanted to work in a much harder level of environment, for example moving from a quiet living room to a crowded public park, it would be helpful to bring the clicker back into the picture.

The clicker is not a remote control. The click comes *after* the correct behavior—it doesn't cause it.

The clicker is not a type of punishment. In fact, it's exactly the opposite. You can think of it as a sort of "I owe you" promise to your dog. To increase a behavior, the reward has to get to your dog within about *two seconds* of the correct behavior. A clicker buys you a bit of extra time by saying "You get a reward for *that* behavior, but give me a moment to bring it to you."

A clicker also makes it easier to move away from having to use food to prompt the behavior in the first place. If you've ever said, "He *knows* it, but he only does it if he can see the cookie!" then you are going to *love* the freedom your clicker gives you.

Can't I Just Say "Yes"?

This is usually the point where someone asks me, "Right, but can't I just say *yes* or *good girl?*"

The short answer is that you can, but I still don't advise it.

There are a few issues with using praise words as your marker.

The first and most important is that your marker is a sacred promise. If you click, you *must* treat. The more reliably your marker predicts the appearance of a reward, the more powerful it becomes as a training tool.

This gets complicated when you're using praise words because honestly, how often do you say the word "yes" or "good" in daily life? If you're anything like me, it's a lot! Every time your dog hears the marker and it isn't followed by a reward, you are removing some of its power as a training tool, so you want to save your marker for something that you'll *only* use in training.

We humans are not terribly conscious of our verbal language. We love to talk, and we love to talk to our dogs, and most of the words that you would automatically gravitate toward as a marker word are also things that you say approximately one zillion times a day.

Separately from that, one of the benefits of using a clicker is that it sounds exactly the same every time. My praise voice doesn't just sound different from your praise voice—it also sounds different from my praise voice earlier this morning or when I had a cold or when I was still slightly irritated with the telemarketer I'd just hung up on, and so on. The clicker allows everyone's "voice" to stay the same in the training context, and that means more clarity for your dog.

And third, a click is just faster, which means it can pinpoint a narrower chunk of behavior, which means you can use it with more precision than a verbal marker. In the time you can say "Good boy," I can click about four times, which means I can be about four times as precise. With a fast dog in particular, that difference adds up quickly!

A faster, more-precise marker means more clarity for your dog, and more clarity means less confusion, and less confusion means less wasted time, which means that your dog gets trained faster.

So while you can use a verbal marker such as "Yes!" instead of a click and get similar results over time, I still strongly recommend the clicker if that's feasible for you.

Charging Your Marker

Have you ever seen a dog who could sleep through a Category 5 hurricane somehow wake up from a dead sleep on the opposite side of the house and come crashing into the kitchen like the Kool-Aid man in half a second flat when a treat bag crinkles?

Then you've seen the power of a conditioned reinforcer in action!

We're going to harness that enthusiasm for the forces of good and get a dog *that* excited about doing their obedience behaviors. Cool, right?

Your dog wasn't born with the understanding that the sound of plastic crinkling was a strong predictor of the arrival of The Good Stuff. Mother Nature did not prepare your dog for crinkly bags as a source of food—you manually installed that. That sound has become a **conditioned reinforcer**, which means it's a previously-neutral noise that has come to have meaning and value by being repeatedly associated with The Good Stuff arriving.

If you wanted, you could use the treat bag crinkling as the marker for your dog's training—it certainly gets a potent response from most dogs! But we're going to create a similar effect with the clicker because that's much more convenient to stick in your pocket and carry around. It's also much harder to accidentally bribe a dog with a clicker instead of rewarding them, whereas there is a definite slippery-slope argument to be made about the crinkly treat bag.

But the end goal is similar: when we click, we want the dog to think, "YIPPEE, I won the lottery!" and look for their treats to immediately appear.

Once we have that, we can be strategic about when we click. Using a clicker to mark exactly the correct moment tells the dog *which* behavior won the lottery, and that encourages them to repeat that behavior again in those circumstances in the future. (Because what's even better than winning the lottery? Knowing the system to win it *again and again!*).

But the first step is to explain to your dog that the clicker means the same thing as the treat bag crinkling: Awesome food will arrive soon.

Are you ready? It's time for your first training exercise. This is an easy one!

Get your dog, your clicker and about thirty treats in your treat pouch.

With your dog in front of you, click the clicker and then give them a treat immediately afterward. Make sure that you don't start to reach for the treat until *after* the sound of the click, but ideally there should be minimal delay.

Wait for a few seconds for your dog to swallow the treat and then repeat the process: click, reach for treat pouch, treat to dog.

During this stage of training, the dog doesn't have to do anything to earn their treats—as long as they're not actively doing something naughty, you can keep going. These freebies are teaching your dog that the click is a strong predictor of The Good Stuff appearing soon.

The Importance of Order

As a quick side note, it's important to make sure that the click is the very first predictor that The Good Stuff is coming.

If your hand is twitching toward the treat pouch like a quick-draw gunslinger *before* the click happens, you're going to erode some of the power of your clicker. Dogs are smart! Your dog is going to tune into that pesky treat hand instead of the clicker—and it's much easier to control a clicker than a hand running on autopilot.

This is a common error, so keep an eye out for it. I've been training professionally for a decade and I still catch myself doing it by accident on occasion.

If this is something you struggle with, it can be helpful to give your treat hand a home base position, such as in your pocket or planted on your leg, and make sure that it's still in home base position before the click.

If you're saying "Yes, good!" before the click, you're not going to get the full benefit of the clicker as a behavior-building tool either. It's an understandable error, but the click needs to be the *first* thing in the sequence, not an afterthought. We're a verbal species and we love to use our words, but for maximum efficacy, they should come *after* the clicker, not before.

So the order should always be: dog does the behavior, click, hand moves to produce treat, and then any optional praise to spice up the reward.

After you've done about thirty pairings of click = treat is coming, you should start to see your dog responding to the sound of the clicker with an expectant or excited response of some sort. Most dogs will look from the clicker toward the treat pouch, or suddenly make eye contact, or seem to startle at the noise of the clicker even though it didn't bother them a minute ago, or freeze sharply and wait for the treat to appear.

We're looking for some sort of noticeable change of behavior where you can see the dog think, "Hey, that noise *means* something."

If you're not seeing that yet, you can practice pairing the clicker and the arrival of The Good Stuff in a few more short sessions, but most dogs will pick it up very quickly. After all, how hard did you have to work to convince them that the sound of the treat bag crinkling was relevant to them?

Marker Timing Drills

Why Timing Matters

We've already talked about why the timing between the click and The Good Stuff appearing is relevant to your dog training. Now we're going to talk about the other side of timing: the timing between the dog's behavior and your click.

The clicker is an incredibly precise tool, and that doesn't do us a bit of good if *we* aren't using it with precision. The tool is only as effective as the skill of the person wielding it—so we're going to build that skill.

Your first responsibility has been to get the treat to the dog in a timely manner after the sound of the click. Now we're going to add your second responsibility: to click at the right time to build the behavior you want.

This comes very naturally to some people and requires more work for others. To prevent any confusion in our dogs, we're going to practice this step without the dog present so you can focus on the people side of the training equation without having to factor in your dog's responses.

Do this exercise with your dog put away in another room. They'll have plenty of time to practice—but right now, it's people-training time.

These exercises are going to hone your ability to click when you mean to click.

You can think of the clicker as a sort of camera to "take pictures" of your dog being good. If you click the shutter of a camera two seconds after the image you wanted to capture, that may or may not make a big difference in the resulting picture. If you're taking a landscape photo using a tripod with a relatively stationary background, maybe that two second gap doesn't make a difference at all. But if you're trying to photograph your kid making the winning goal at their first ever soccer match and you click the camera two seconds late, you've probably just wasted the photo—and completely missed the memory you were trying to capture.

Dog training? Same.

If you have a relatively chill dog who takes a while to move between behaviors and you're working on a longer-duration behavior like building a stay, some minor timing errors are unlikely to be the end of the world. But if you've got a fast dog or a puppy or you're working on a behavior that really matters to you, it absolutely pays to be precise.

Plus, the exercises are secretly fun!

Clicker Timing Exercises: Tennis Ball and TV

The two classic clicker timing exercises will require a tennis ball and a TV. (Yes, those are official dog training supplies.)

We're going to start with the tennis ball so you can use your ears as well as your eyes.

Start off with the tennis ball in one and your clicker in the other.

This exercise is easiest if you start off standing up, but for a more advanced version, you can repeat the same game sitting down.

Drop the tennis ball toward the ground from shoulder height, and with your other hand, try to click your clicker the exact moment that the tennis ball hits the ground. This works best if you're practicing on a non-carpeted, non-grass surface so you can actually hear the sound of the tennis ball bouncing on the floor.

Did the bounce happen at the same time as your click?

Repeat this until you're able to reliably capture the moment that your tennis ball strikes the ground—the sound of the bounce and the click should at least partially overlap. It takes some coordination in the beginning, but that's why we're practicing without the dog! When you can get eight out of ten correct, you're ready to move on.

The second exercise is more advanced because you have less time to prepare to click and you have to be able to respond quickly.

Turn on the television (or Netflix or YouTube, for the millennials like me without a real TV) and get your clicker ready. Turn on a show you're not really interested in for its own sake—you're using this as a training exercise, not watching TV for fun. For the next five minutes, try to click the moment that the scene changes. This isn't as obvious as when a ball will strike the ground, so it will take a lot more focus to get your timing right and it's normal to have a higher rate of errors on this step, especially at first.

For the TV exercise, the goal isn't to be perfect. You're just trying to flex your timing muscles and your ability to predict a behavior. Are you starting to notice patterns that predict when the scene is about to change? Are you usually clicking too early or too late?

Exercises like this will help you hone your ability to click exactly when your dog does the right behavior, and will dramatically speed up your training progress. If you're a sharpshooter with clicking the TV exercises, you'll have top-notch precision when teaching your dog—but as long as you're able to click the ball hitting the ground most of the time, you're ready to move onto the next section.

Why Delivery Matters

The next thing we're going to practice is delivering food to the dog when and where we mean to.

The place where the food appears makes a surprising amount of difference in your dog training efficacy. You can supercharge your progress by using your reinforcer delivery in a thoughtful way that supports your training goals.

I like to think of my food delivery as adding a sort of magnet to the place where the dog meets the food. It's not a stuck-there-forever kind of magnet, but it still has a meaningful amount of influence, just enough to slowly nudge things in the direction that the magnet pulls.

Dogs are masters of efficiency. If you reward directly in front of your knees, dogs are going to take the most efficient route between the end of the behavior they were doing to earn the click and the front of your knees. And the more predictable you are about putting the reinforcer in the same place every time, the stronger that effect is going to be.

You can see this in action if you pick up your dog's leash in the middle of the house and your dog immediately bolts to the door instead of coming to you to have the leash put on. The door is the gateway to the reinforcement that the leash has promised, so dogs are cutting out the middleman and going straight to the source.

During our training together, we're going to take advantage of this tendency in order to create stronger behaviors, and just like with the clicker timing, we're going to practice the human half of the equation before adding the dog into the picture.

Our goal in these exercises is to get very good at putting the food exactly where we want it to go so that skill is on autopilot once we start adding in more factors like the dog's movement and paying attention to the environment.

Food Delivery Exercises

We're going to practice three different basic delivery positions, although you are welcome and encouraged to expand from here if you'd like.

For the purposes of these exercises, you're going to need a bowl as a substitute dog. You'll also need some sort of raised surface like a table or upside down cardboard box at approximately the same height as your dog's head. Close enough is close enough, but try to get in the same ballpark as your dog's height (e.g., if you have a chihuahua, don't use a table).

Start off with your bowl directly in front of your body at the height of your dog's face. This front delivery position is going to be the easiest and most natural for most people.

Click, then quickly drop a treat into the bowl with your other hand.

The bowl represents your dog's face. We're using a specific target because I want you to get into the habit of putting the treat where you intend for it to go, not meeting your dog halfway. For most of our training, you'll be delivering the treat to a specific place and we want your dog to adjust their behavior based on where the treat appears—so get into the habit of putting the treat where you *want* the dog to be and trusting the dog to show up there.

Practice this until you feel like you've gotten as fast as you're going to get. Then set a timer for one minute and count how many treats you're able to get into a bowl before the timer goes off. Aim for at least ten, but more is better.

Then pivot 90 degrees so the dog-face-height bowl is now beside your left leg. This is going to be your heel position delivery when we start working on leash skills. Practice this placement the same as the front delivery and be patient with yourself in the process. You probably have less practice with the heel position delivery than delivering a treat directly in front of you, so it's normal for it to feel a bit awkward at first. This version is easiest if you have the clicker in your right hand and the treats on your left.

Make sure your feet stay planted and you aren't slowly shifting to face the bowl. For most dogs, the bowl should be roughly aligned with your left knee.

Click, twist and deliver the treat to the bowl on your left. Straighten your back before you click for the next repetition so you don't stay twisted sideways for the whole exercise. It should feel like a weird sort of yoga exercise or disco dance move: twist and straighten, twist and straighten.

Practice this until the awkwardness wears off and it starts to feel normal, then set your timer again. Can you match the number of treats-per-minute that you could deliver to front position?

And finally, place the bowl on the ground about a foot in front of you and practice dropping treats into the bowl. This will be your floor delivery. I am less picky with precision on a floor delivery because treats bounce differently on different types of flooring and you'll make yourself crazy if you try to account for all of that as a beginner, but it's worth practicing to get the treats in the ballpark of where you want them to go. Gradually step away from the bowl and toss treats toward it from a variety of angles. If you've ever played horseshoes, this should feel pretty similar. You don't need to work up to any crazy distances, but get comfortable with landing treats in the bowl from a couple of steps away. No big deal if the treat bounces out of the bowl or lands right beside it.

Now you have your three main delivery positions: front, heel and floor.

Next, bring your dog into the room and practice each food delivery position with your dog. They will love this step—free treats!

It's normal to go significantly slower at first when you add a real dog into the equation because there's an extra body's motion to account for. Make sure that you are deliberate about which reward delivery you're going to use. Remember that the dog should move toward the treat, not the other way around—put the treat in the correct position and trust your dog to appear there. If your dog is standing six inches off center in front, stick to your guns and hold the treat directly in front position. If they want the treat (and they *do* want the treat, don't they?), they'll move to where you're delivering it.

This is the last of the basic mechanics exercises.

Now you've worked through the component pieces. Your dog knows that clicking means a treat is coming. You know how to click when you intend to click and put food where you intend to put food. These are the fundamental building blocks of dog training. The rest of dog training is just both of you combining those skills in specific ways.

Contextual Learners

Starting In Kindergarten

A few last points before we dive into your dog's obedience education for real.

With each exercise we teach, we're going to be starting in the easiest possible environment. We want minimal distractions and maximum environmental control so that your dog can focus on their learning without having to filter out a lot of extra things. For most families, that means we're going to start teaching everything in the living room at a quiet time of day.

If you're training multiple dogs, you're still going to teach each one individually, even if they're best buddies. Any kids or pets who aren't actively involved in the training should ideally be in another room or otherwise occupied and unlikely to interfere. The training environment doesn't need to be entirely sterile, but don't make it any harder than it has to be. The harder your dog has to work to focus on you, the harder the skills will be for him to learn and the more repetitions you're going to need to do before he gets it, so it pays off to make it easy at first.

"But wait! My dog lives in the real world and the real world has distractions!"

Absolutely true, and we're going to get to that stage later in the training. We don't send five-year-olds to college calculus classes because "the real world has calculus" and we're not going to do it to your dog either. We're going to start in kindergarten, and that means a low-distraction, familiar environment where your dog can focus on their education. The real world will still be there when they're ready.

"Going back to kindergarten" is a theme we're going to work with a lot. I believe credit for that phrase goes to Canadian dog trainer Sue Ailsby, but I love it and I'm borrowing it. There's no shame in going back to an easier situation to shore up a wobbly skill before taking it back into the real world and I want you to feel comfortable with working on the baby-beginner level of each behavior, even things that your dog already knows.

Just like we broke down the clicker training mechanics in the last chapter, we're going to break down your dog's obedience behaviors into simple pieces and gradually assemble them into a more impressive whole.

The process of breaking the skills down into their component parts is called **splitting** (and failing to do so is **lumping,** asking for too much difficulty too soon). In our training, we always want to be good splitters and look for the smallest pieces that the behavior can be reduced to, then assemble the rest of the skill around that. It'll make more sense once you've practiced it hands-on, but for now, trust me that we're starting in the living room and not in the middle of the neighborhood park or wherever your dog's behavior issues are happening.

Boredom? I Don't Think So

In addition to starting in a low-distraction environment such as a boring living room, we're also going to keep our training sessions short, targeted and highly reinforcing. No one likes a teacher who drones on and on, and that includes dogs!

In the beginning, you want each training session to run about five minutes, and sometimes even less. If you're like me and you have a tendency to lose track of time when you're having fun, feel free to set a timer to keep yourself honest—you'll be amazed how fast it actually is!

In addition to structured lessons, I love to use the empty pockets of time in my day that I would otherwise waste. I keep some non-refrigerated treats ready to go near my microwave so I can work on something quick with the dog while I'm waiting for the microwave to ding. It's not like I was going to do anything else useful with that time. Likewise, if you watch any type of media with commercials, practice a few obedience behaviors with the dog during the commercial break.

It may seem counterintuitive to limit yourself to short training sessions, especially if you have a very smart dog, a very eager dog or a very naughty dog who needs help ASAP. But you'll actually make faster progress working in repeated short bursts than you'd make if you drilled for half an hour.

Keeping the sessions short and minimizing distractions also gives us an extra gift: a diagnostic.

If your dog is in an undistracting environment and has the ability to earn fabulous rewards during a very short period of time for a tiny amount of thinking, he'd have to be nuts to choose to ignore you or "get bored." You've stacked the deck in your favor—you're the best game in town, guaranteed!

On the one hand, that makes training go faster because you're the most appealing option in the room and mama didn't raise no fool.

And on the other hand, if your dog *does* disengage with you and decide that they'd rather not train right now, thanks, then that is crucial information to have.

Nine and a half times out of ten, as long as you have a reinforcer that they actually want, a dog walking away from easy treats means that you're asking for more behavior than your dog is capable of giving you and they are frustrated. It's not "an attitude" and it's not "deciding they don't have to do it." If this is happening on a regular basis, it's time to go back to kindergarten on that skill *no matter how well you think they know it*, because your dog's behavior is telling you they're not ready yet.

Think of it this way:

Imagine that we are in a boring waiting room and you've got nothing better to do.

I have a $100 bill. You know that I have a $100 bill. If I asked you to perform a basic behavior like touching the top of your head or tying your shoes and said I would pay you the entire $100 the first time you did it, no strings attached, what *possible* incentive could you have to not comply? You don't lose anything by participating and you get a hundred bucks.

If you said, "No thanks, I'd rather watch paint dry," that would be a pretty big deal. There would have to be something seriously wrong with our communication (do we speak the same language?), or you'd need to know the $100 was a counterfeit ("Nice try, but that's a $1 that someone drew two zeroes on with a sharpie!"), or there would need to be some sort of environmental stressor (are we in line at the bank during an active robbery?), or something like that.

If you catch yourself saying, "He's just bored" or "He's so *stubborn*" or "But he *knows* this," I want you to ask yourself why your dog would walk away from a $100 bill and I want you to be honest when you answer.

When to Move On

"So, when do we get to move on from kindergarten? There are other grades and there's a whole world out there for my dog to learn about!"

Patience, grasshopper! We'll get to the real world soon enough—in fact, there's a whole section in this book on how to level up these skills in a systematic and reliable way. But for now, we're going to talk about the SparkNotes version until you get there.

In positive reinforcement training, we want to set up the challenges so our dog is right almost all of the time. There's no need for your dog to get it wrong, and contrary to common perception, your dog doesn't need to know what behaviors are bad in order to choose the behaviors that are good. We're going to try to keep our dogs on the right track as much as possible, which means we're going to raise the difficulty level only when we're very sure that they can *already* do the next step.

What that means in practice is that you don't want to move on until your dog is getting it right at least 80% of the time at this level, and ideally more than that. If you drop below about an 80% success rate, that means your dog is struggling and could use some support from you to get it right. And if they get it wrong more than twice in a row, that should be a red flag that you may be pushing too fast. You want the dog to be right almost all of the time, and if that means taking a short trip back to kindergarten for a refresher, that's perfectly acceptable. What is *not* acceptable is continuing to ask for a behavior that your dog is showing you they can't do right now.

And it's worth pointing out that the environment is a huge factor in this. The fact that your dog can sit on cue in the living room does not mean that they can do it just as easily in the kitchen. Dogs are contextual learners, which means they get an A+ in learning specifics and more like a D in generalizations. They're excellent at learning to differentiate things and significantly less good at "Dude, it's the exact same thing." The vast majority of the time when someone tells me that their dog *knows* this behavior but he's just "being stubborn," the issue boils down to a dog who learned a skill in one specific context and failed to pick up the general principle, such as a dog who is house trained in one location but not in others, or a dog who never gets in the trash at home but thinks grandma's trash can is fair game.

We're going to address all of those things later in the book, *promise*, but in the short term, we're going to focus on working where our dog can be successful and only leveling up their training when they show us that they're ready. You can think of it as a sort of canine Montessori school—learner-directed training. If your dog is ready to do this skill in a more challenging environment, they'll show you!

2

Skill Building

Offered Versus Cued Attention

Hooray, Your First Training Exercise!

"Phew, enough theory! Let's get to the training!"

I hear you and I admire your enthusiasm. Let's get started!

For our first exercise, you'll need a small supply of pea-sized treats, a treat pouch, your clicker and your dog.

We're going to teach the foundation skill of dog training for you *and* your dog. Your dog is going to learn how to pay attention to you, and at the same time, you are going to learn how to pay attention to your dog.

I know that sounds a little patronizing, but dog-training attention and regular attention are two totally different beasts, and I believe in starting in kindergarten for the people end of the leash too.

Also, I should mention that when I say pea-sized training treats, I'm talking about something that your dog is really into. Put away those dried up old biscuits, and for that matter, most commercially produced dog treats. That's doggie minimum wage and we want to pay our learners what they're worth. If you pay with minimum wage treats, you're going to get minimum wage results. Go ahead and be generous.

I like to use a sort of trail mix of my dogs' regular dinner kibble, some tiny (*tiny*) hotdog slices and some tiny pieces of cheese, but your dog's preferences may vary. I choose those because they tend to have strong scents which mix with the kibble to sort of upgrade the value of the kibble itself.

I'm also a huge fan of the dog treat brand Happy Howie's, which is what I use for most of my training with clients—the turkey rolls in particular are a big hit. The rolls need to be refrigerated and you have to cut the treats yourself, but it's a pretty good bargain if you'd feel more comfortable buying something that's labeled as a dog treat. Just get into the habit of storing your treat pouch in the fridge if you use anything that needs to be refrigerated and give it a quick wash as needed for hygiene purposes.

Go ahead and stock your treat pouch with about a meal's worth of The Good Stuff, whatever that looks like for your dog today. If your dog isn't begging just a little bit when they smell what you've got in the pouch, it's probably not high enough value. You want something they're really willing to put forth some effort for. Don't be a stingy boss if you can avoid it.

My Pet Peeve About "Watch Me"

"Watch me" is one of the first behaviors taught in a lot of obedience classes and given the title of this chapter, you'll probably be surprised to learn that it's one of my biggest pet peeves. This is because of the way it's traditionally taught.

The way that it's traditionally taught goes something like this:

The owner puts a treat in front of the dog's face and then rapidly lifts it to the person's eyes. The dog's gaze follows the treat, because "Oh my god, she has *treats!*" and they accidentally look at their handler's eyes in the process, or at least in the vicinity. The owner clicks and gives the dog the treat. Repeat ad nauseum, eventually adding in the cue "Watch me!" before moving the treat.

Not going to pull punches here: I hate it.

This makes initiating eye contact entirely the human's responsibility. I don't know about you, but I don't want to have to specifically *ask* my dog to acknowledge that I exist for the next decade or two. I don't want to be the eye contact enforcer and I feel pretty squicky about the whole "is the dog looking at the treat or is the dog looking at my face" business too.

And it often leads to people desperately chanting "watch me, watch me, watch me" at a dog who is completely oblivious at the other end of a leash because the environment is too much for them to handle and everything about their body language makes it blindingly obvious that they are not in a learning frame of mind.

You don't wanna be that guy.

If you're having to beg your dog to look at you, this environment is way too hard for your dog's current skill level and trying to mask it by putting a cookie under your dog's nose is not helping you in the long run.

I am (hopefully obviously) not anti-cookie, nor even anti-luring, but with eye contact in particular, I refuse.

Eye contact is a canary-in-a-coal-mine behavior for me. It's a diagnostic, a check-engine light. If I'm not getting eager eye contact from my dog, that tells me that something is *wrong*. I teach my dogs to initiate eye contact for the same reason that I keep batteries in my smoke detector (even though it yells at me for cooking dinner drastically more often than it saves me from legitimate house fires).

Eye contact should be an indicator of attention, not a behavior we paste onto a distracted dog. Even if I got eye contact by waving treats at my dog and luring their gaze up to me, that does me absolutely zero good if my dog's *brain* isn't also focusing on me, which that treat is likely to be masking.

So come on, guys, your dog is smarter than that. Let's give them a

little credit!
And a little responsibility to go with it.

Attention Is the Dog's Choice

From now on, it's your dog's job to keep their attention on you.

And on the flip side, you don't get to ask for it or demand it. If you find yourself having to ask for their attention repeatedly, you haven't been doing your real jobs. *Your* only jobs are to manage the situation so they are likely to *choose* to give you their attention and then to pay for their attention when they give it to you.

In other words, the dog is the one in the driver's seat for this skill. If you do it right, they will be *shoving* their eye contact at you and being obnoxiously attentive, which is an excellent problem to have in the long run even if it's a bit comical in the beginning. Pretty much no one hires a dog trainer because their dog pays *too* much attention to them, you know?

This is one of those paradigm shifts that kills a bunch of birds with one stone. Ready?

It's not your responsibility to force your dog to do the behavior that you want them to do—it's your responsibility to make it worth their effort so your dog will *choose* to initiate that behavior on their own in hopes that you'll pay up (which you will, at least some of the time).

If you've ever groaned that your dog only wants to listen if they think it was their idea in the first place, you're gonna *love* this stuff.

By teaching your dog that it is *their* job to stay engaged with you, instead of constantly nagging them to acknowledge your existence, you can build in a robust diagnostic. If your dog knows that paying attention to you pays well for dogs, and if your dog is choosing not to pay attention to you even though that is an easy win that requires basically no effort from them whatsoever, then that tells you that they're not in a thinking frame of mind and trying to teach them when they're overwhelmed isn't likely to get you very far.

If they can't give you eye contact, they can't give you much else either and it becomes your job to make the environment easier so the dog can think.

If you've ever felt the difference between a dog who is only about 10% sure that there's even a living person attached to the other end of his leash and a dog with such solid focus on you that you couldn't pry their gaze off your face with a crowbar, it's no contest. You want the attentive one.

And as a nice bonus, it's dead easy to teach and a great intro behavior for training for both ends of the leash, which is why we're starting here.

We want this to be one of your dog's go-to behaviors. That way, when they're not sure what's going on, one of their default settings is "What if I just made eye contact and checked in with you? Would that work?"

Well, sure! That's almost never going to be the wrong choice.

As a side note, this is going to make your leash walking and your come-when-called skills about a zillion times easier too, because it's much easier to keep a dog close to you if they already have a rich learning history for checking in.

Learning to See the Good

If you're like most of the dog owners I work with, your "puppy vision" is on point. You're probably very good at noticing when your dog is misbehaving or hearing when the house is suspiciously quiet—*too* quiet.

But outside of formal training sessions, most of the people I work with don't have a lot of experience with noticing their dog being good.

So the first lesson for both ends of the leash is going to build that skill.

Hold your clicker in one hand and a treat in the other, with your hands held neutrally at your side. You may need to hold them behind your back at first if you have an enthusiastic learner who is leaping at your hands—that's fine and we'll fix it later. Be ready to click.

The second your dog makes eye contact with you, click immediately and hand them the treat as quickly as you can. Remember that the click comes *first*. This is the promise that The Good Stuff is coming and it should precisely mark the behavior you want to reward: in this case, a split second of eye contact. The treat can be a second or two later, but try to get it to them as quickly as you can as long as it's after the click.

Reload the treat hand and repeat.

It's normal for your dog to stare at the treat hand, sniff the floor or seem distracted. It usually passes in about fifteen seconds (but feels like approximately fifty years when you're new to this). *Do not help the dog.* Do not cough conspicuously or make little noises to get their attention or shuffle your feet just a bit to help them. *Resist.*

Eventually, and usually within fewer than twenty seconds, your dog will happen to glance up at your eyes again, even just for a split second.

Click! And then treat again. Reload your treat hand.

As you repeat this, I want you to also pay attention to the time in between the reps. For most dogs, the gaps between treats start to diminish within just a few repetitions—around twenty seconds at first, then ten, then only five or so as they start to get into the flow. Five seconds between reps is a pretty good place to be.

Usually after about ten repetitions, you'll see a little lightbulb go off in the dog's brain. "Wait. Could it possibly be this simple? Am I *making* this happen?!" You'll often see a very deliberate glance up and a small freeze, like "Did it *work?*"

Yes it did! Click, pay, reload.

That lightbulb moment is the point of this exercise. Once your dog has been paid for that a handful of times, their eye contact should become more pointed and faster. "I did it, pay me. I did it again, pay me again. Wow, I could keep looking at you *all day*. How many treats do you have?"

Practice this for about three minutes, then end the session. You want to end when they still think this is the easiest game they've ever played in their life—don't be tempted to get greedy and train until the dog quits on you.

Congratulations! You're already one step closer to a more attentive, obedient dog and you barely had to lift a finger! This exercise may be simple, but it's ridiculously useful and it's going to make your relationship with your dog so much better as you level it up.

Hands Off, Mouth Closed

For a lot of people, this is not going to feel very much like training at all, especially if you've experienced old-school training before this.

After all, you didn't touch the dog and you never said a word. How is that going to help you at all in the real world? How will the dog know what you want if you don't give them *commands?*

The secret is that most good dog training is "hands off, mouth closed" in the beginning and a lot of it stays that way. If you do a good enough job with training, you can create a dog who does what you want without you even having to ask for it. And wouldn't that be convenient?

Sure, we'll add verbal cues to plenty of their obedience behaviors so you can ask for them when you want them, but a lot of the skills we're going to build in this book are going to become your dog's default settings, and you don't usually ask for defaults. It still counts as training and it's often much more powerful than the types of behaviors you ask for.

In this case, I rarely bother to add an explicit verbal cue for attention.

If my dog can't find my eyes on his own without my help, that's all the information I need. In other words, I am rarely going to need eye contact *alone*. If I want a sit and eye contact, I'm just going to ask for the sit because the attention is still the dog's responsibility.

For future behaviors, rest assured, we're going to use verbal cues. Your dog is going to learn plenty of ways to behave politely on autopilot, but we're going to install some buttons for you to push when you want a specific behavior too.

But in general, there's going to be a lot of quiet in this dog training and that's intentional.

When you're teaching a new behavior, your dog is focusing on their behavior and the consequence it produces. If you add the command at this point, you're just muddying the water and distracting them. It *feels* like you're helping, but you're not. Humans are a very verbal species; we like our words. Dogs are more interested in the outcome. Did the treat appear? When? Where? On what contingency? Your only job at first is to produce the consequence—in this case, a click and a treat when your dog successfully finds your eyes.

Once your dog is offering the behavior almost on loop, we'll help them out and tell them what that behavior is called, but we're not there yet.

Trusting the Process

Your homework for this exercise is simple: I want you to trust the process.

At least three times a day for the next week or so, I want you to practice this exercise around the house with your dog. You can super-charge it by practicing right before your dog's normal meals, walks or something else that they strongly anticipate every day, but any time will do. Don't feel like you need to drill for an extended period of time—five minutes at a time is *plenty* and maybe even too much depending on the dog.

Remember that choosing to make eye contact is your dog's responsibility and reinforcement is yours. Their job is to look at you and your job is to pay them for it.

During this week, I want you to keep an eye on a couple of things.

First, pay attention to the amount of time in between your dog swallowing the treat and your dog initiating eye contact again. This loop should get smaller and smaller over time until your dog is staring at you almost as soon as they've finished swallowing.

That's great! That tells you that they are beginning to understand that their behavior controls the click and the click controls the treat. The stronger their understanding that their behavior produces the treat, the faster they're going to learn everything else. It's okay if it feels a little bit like they are "taking advantage" or "manipulating you" to get treats—you *want* that. That's not a bug, it's a feature!

And second, I want you to start to notice how often your dog initiates eye contact during the rest of your day-to-day life. If they're like most dogs, that should start to become more frequent. It'll be gradual, but there if you look for it. The more often you pay for it, the more often they choose to offer it. Even if you're not in the middle of a formal training session, feel free to pay them for choosing to make eye contact and check in with you (unless it happens in a situation where you never want them to pay attention to you, such as begging at the table—those you can ignore). The more often that behavior pays off for them in a variety of situations, the more likely it is to become their go-to behavior and the more attentive they're going to become over time.

When your dog is getting really good at this game and you are ready to raise the difficulty level a bit, start dropping the treat between your feet after the click instead of delivering it straight to your dog's mouth. This is the first step of what I call the "get lost and come back" game.

You encourage the dog to "get lost" by dropping the treat so they have to move their attention all the way away from you to find it on the floor and eat it. Then when they re-engage with you and make eye contact again, you pay them for "coming back" by dropping another treat.

You don't need to throw the food far at all—right between your feet is fine, and I wouldn't go much farther than two feet away from you even for an advanced dog. You just lose more time on sniffing but you don't get much more benefit on the come-back part, so it's fine to keep them pretty close to you.

Next, we're going to work on the first step of teaching your dog to come when called.

Targeting: Hand Target

What Is Targeting?

Targeting is the dog training version of duct tape—it's easy, it's cheap and it holds things together. And just like duct tape, it doesn't look like much at first, but you can fix an awful lot of problems with this super simple skill!

At its most general, targeting is teaching an animal to connect This to That.

For example, teaching a dog to go to their crate is technically a target: connect your whole body to the bottom of your crate.

Teaching a heel is mobile targeting: connect the right side of your shoulder to the left side of my leg and stay connected even when my leg is moving.

And if you've ever taught a dog to shake hands, congratulations! You've taught a dog to connect their paw to your hand on cue—the textbook example of a beginner paw target.

Targeting is useful because it gives the dog a very specific behavior to perform and typically a prop of some sort to glue the behavior together (in the previous examples: a crate, your leg and your hand).

What Does a Hand Target Look Like?

For this lesson, we're going to teach the most iconic type of target and in my opinion one of the most useful skills a dog can learn: a hand target.

Or as the kids are saying these days: a snoot boop.

(Yes, your cue can be "boop," and yes, it is every bit as adorable as you just thought.)

The goal of this behavior is for your dog to connect the tip of their nose to the palm of your hand when you ask. We'll start off very close to the dog so they would almost have to try to get it wrong, then gradually increase the distance until your magnetic hand can summon your dog from all the way across the house.

And where the dog's nose goes, the rest of the dog will follow—which means you'll also get a casual come-when-called as a freebie.

How to Teach a Hand Target

One of the best things about a hand target is that for most dogs, this behavior comes partially pre-installed by Mother Nature. That makes it a great beginner exercise to work with!

Begin with your clicker in one hand and quickly present the other hand right beside your dog's nose.

It's important to start off closer than you would think! You want your hand to be as close to your dog's face as possible without actually touching it—the dog should barely have to move at all.

Perfect positioning is about an inch away from your dog's nose and oriented diagonally alongside your dog's muzzle at about a 45 degree angle (rather than stop-sign straight across the front of their nose or parallel along their muzzle). If you imagine shaking hands with the tips of your dog's whiskers, that's exactly the position you want.

If your dog is like 90% of dogs, they'll go, "Hey, what's that?" and turn to see why you've stuck your hand in their face… and bump their nose into your palm in the process by accident.

Click the second they touch your hand! And quickly give them a treat with the same hand you just used as the target.

Next, repeat this several times at this distance until your dog is happily anticipating the next time they'll be able to push the invisible treat-button in your hand with their nose. In the beginning, it is completely okay if your dog pokes your hand seemingly by accident rather than on purpose. As long as the dog was the one who touched you and not the other way around, it counts!

But resist the urge to reach out and touch the dog instead. You can do all of the moving up to about an inch away from their muzzle, but the last inch is your dog's job.

Troubleshooting

Don't worry if they leave you hanging for a few seconds of awkward silence. That's pretty normal with a beginner dog and it'll work out over time. This skill may start off hesitant, but it tends to build momentum very quickly, so your dog will be a nose targeting champion in no time!

If you're worried about it or if you feel like your dog is particularly stuck, you can rotate your wrist slightly outward away from your dog, as if moving partially from a straight up and down handshake position in the beginning to a palm-upward receive-gift position. For some dogs, this reduces the spatial pressure and it's easier for them to move toward you if your hand very slightly retreats from them first.

For other dogs, it can be very helpful to look at your hand rather than staring at your dog—especially if you've just been training eye contact in the last chapter. Dogs are masters of body language and they're great at moving where your body language suggests they should be. If you're staring straight at them but your hand is off to the side, they'll usually stay centered in front of you. But if you look toward your own hand and orient your shoulders toward your target hand, nine times out of ten, the dog will move in that direction too.

Remember that at this point, we're not talking to the dog or touching the dog first. Your dog is learning how to use their behavior to "force" you to click and treat them. And every time they touch your hand with their nose, even if it's by accident, they get an immediate click and a treat.

It helps to build some momentum with this skill so they are able to rapid-fire poke your hand as soon as it's available, so if the skill is still looking a little sluggish, keep working on it at the easy level until your dog is absolutely nailing it. This should be a behavior that your dog is thrilled to do! When you're ready to move on, there should be a sort of continuous rhythm to it: poke-click-treat-poke-click-treat.

Once your dog is consistently and enthusiastically bumping their nose into your hand at the first opportunity, you can start gradually making the distance or angle more difficult.

Raise the difficulty slowly here—like *really* slowly. We're talking like an inch at a time, just enough that they have to giraffe-neck. Sprinkle in a few easy repetitions too so they don't get discouraged. Gradually build up until your dog is able to move about a foot from side to side to nose-poke your hand, and pay for each repetition.

To raise the difficulty again once they're a pro at the last step, instead of handing the treat to your dog as they stand or sit in front of you, try tossing the treat a foot or so off to the side onto the floor. It doesn't need to be far—just enough to get your dog moving a step or two away from you.

After they've gotten that treat, as they turn and start to move back toward you, present your other hand in target position right in the middle of their path of travel—so you almost "catch" them with your target hand as they walk back to you. When they nose-target your hand, toss a treat in the direction your dog was already moving.

If you repeat this, your dog should be basically walking back and forth in front of you—picking up a treat to your right, poking your left hand in the middle, picking up another treat on the left, poking your right hand in the middle, and so on.

When they're in this pattern, you can start to hold your hand farther and farther away on the path of travel so they have to deliberately move into your hand to trigger the next treat. For example, toss the treat off to your left, then lean with your arm all the way out to the right so they have to go past your whole body to get to your hand. This is the beginning step of adding distance to your hand target. As your dog's skill develops, you can toss their treat farther and farther away so they have to work harder to press the target the next time.

After your dog is a pro at targeting back and forth on the path in front of you, you can start to gradually build up the distance by tossing the treat as before, waiting for the dog to pick up the tossed treat and jogging a step or two away from the dog before presenting the hand target again. Most dogs *love* this game and will enthusiastically chase your retreating target hand to boop it for another treat—and you're secretly practicing the beginning steps of coming when called.

When Will I Ever Use This?

A hand target may seem like a cute trick, but it's one of the most useful foundation behaviors you can teach. When a new puppy comes into my house, the three skills we work on first are a hand target (move toward me), a leave it (move away from that) and a go to bed (stop moving). With those three skills alone, you can solve a remarkable amount of puppy mischief!

To give you an idea of how useful a hand target is, I ask my dogs for a target about three times as often as I ask for a sit—it's *that* useful!

So, when can you use it?

The most common use for a hand target is that it builds nicely into a come-when-called behavior—because of course the rest of the dog is attached to the nose, which is now attached to your hand. Your dog can't poke your hand without also coming close to you.

It's also a very low-pressure way to move your dog through space. Instead of shooing your dog off the sofa with spatial pressure or taking them by the collar, you can present a low hand target to encourage them to jump off on their own. If they're standing in exactly the wrong space in the kitchen while you're trying to cook (and I swear, they have an *uncanny* ability to be in exactly the wrong space in the kitchen, don't they?), you can present a hand target off to the side to ask them to move out of your way instead of barging through them or walking around them. If you need them to jump into the car or get onto the scale at the vet, ask for a hand target—and so on. It's a polite way to ask your dog to move instead of physically moving them around.

It also tends to be a cheap behavior, so I can use this to test to ask, "Hey pup, how much brain do you have in this environment?"

Capturing: Default Sit

What Is Capturing?

Capturing is a method of training that allows your dog to take the driver's seat. Instead of focusing on what commands to give or how to prompt the behavior to happen, capturing involves waiting for the desired behavior to happen and making it pay off for the dog when it happens.

It sounds too simple to be effective, but this stuff is magic!

I mean, let's think about it. Almost every problem behavior that you want to fix with your dog was initially taught via capturing. Nature *loves* capturing. If you've ever groaned that your relative fed the dog from the table *one time* and now the dog spends every meal time staring holes into your dinner plate in hopes of scraps, then you've seen the power of capturing in real life. Likewise if your dog got into the trash *one time* and suddenly became a garbage-eating Houdini who could work their way through Fort-Knox-level security to feast on trash, or if your dog successfully pulls on the leash to get where they're going, and so on.

One of the biggest and most damaging myths in dog training is the mistaken belief that the power is in the commands. Your command could be literally anything. It could be "sofa cushion" or "ceiling fan" or "butts." The real magic of dog training is in the consequences: what consequence does the dog unlock with this behavior? And capturing is an awesome crash course in how consequences work to build reliable behaviors.

Why Is Capturing Amazing?

As far as I'm concerned, capturing is the unsung hero of dog training and one of the most effective methods of building new behaviors.

Captured behaviors tend to pick up a lot of momentum very quickly, which is what makes them so frustrating when you're working with naturally-developed behaviors that you *don't* want to maintain (such as the trash-scavenging or begging at the table above).

Capturing is super easy for the dogs because it's how they naturally learn, so there's very little "installation" required in the process of building the behavior. The eye contact game we played in the previous chapter was an early example of capturing: you waited for the dog to initiate the behavior by looking at you, then paid for it.

If you've ever potty trained a dog by praising them when they go potty outside on grass, then congratulations, you have already successfully captured a behavior—which I'm willing to bet is pretty sturdy if you have an adult dog. And because you've also linked that behavior to an environmental consequence (in this case, the relief of an empty bladder), you probably have a self-sustaining behavior at this point. I'm going to go out on a limb and guess that you haven't put a lot of thought into praising your dog for their bathroom habits since they were a younger puppy.

The hardest thing about capturing is setting up the environment to make it likely for the behavior to happen naturally in the first place—for example, don't try to capture a relaxed down in the middle of the dog park or you're going to be waiting for a while.

The second hardest part is trusting the process and keeping your mouth shut so the dog can think. (But I say that kindly and with love.)

In the long term, captured behaviors tend to become your dog's go-to behaviors when they don't know what behavior to offer, which is why we're going to choose behaviors that are very unlikely to become obnoxious if the dog starts spamming us with that behavior. We absolutely do not want to capture demand behaviors such as barking, pawing, nose poking or invading our physical space, because those behaviors can be unpleasant, and in some cases dangerous or painful, if the dog does them when we're not expecting them. So when we choose capturing to build behavior, we want to pick behaviors that are pretty unlikely to be a problem if the dog does them whenever.

It's worth adding that one click or one treat does not typically buy you a full behavior forever. The joke is that single-trial learning only happens for the behaviors you never want to see again, and it takes considerably more behavioral momentum to build the behaviors that you want. Captured behaviors tend to build momentum and snowball into stronger and stronger behaviors over time, so we're going to repeatedly upvote the same behaviors to increase their frequency in the dog's repertoire.

Teaching Your Dog to Be Stubbornly Good

My favorite thing about capturing is that it is excellent at teaching dogs to be "stubbornly good," by which I mean that it can build very sturdy default behaviors which are resistant to temptation or outside interference.

A place where I see a disconnect between modern training and old-school training is the way that we teach good behaviors. Old-school dog training treated good behavior as the opposite of wrong, and if you removed all of the wrong (via punishment), you'd have a good dog underneath it. Modern dog training takes a totally different approach: our goal is to make the good behavior inherently desirable so the dog is absolutely thrilled to do the behavior that you want them to do.

At the end of the day, dogs do what works. If being "naughty" works, they will continue to do that, because it continues to work.

But if we can get ahead of that and teach the dog that the behavior we want them to do is a much faster and more reliable path to reinforcement, we can shift the entire trajectory of their behavior without having to suppress them or punish them or scold them. It makes showing them what's wrong obsolete.

Instead, we can show them that the behavior we don't want them to do is just plain inefficient. Dogs are *masters* of efficiency.

As we reinforce the behaviors we'd like to see more of, they start to calcify and gain strength. The more reliably these behaviors pay off, the more reliably our dogs will do them—in which case our job is just to point a neon sign at the behavior we *do* want the dogs to do and then prove to them that it works better (from the dog's point of view) than the behavior that would have otherwise been their go-to.

I call this teaching dogs to be stubbornly good. I want a dog who *insists* on doing the behavior that I want them to do because darn it, *this* is how I can make The Good Stuff happen.

And the cool thing is that just like us, dogs have only twenty-four hours of behavior in a day. If we upvote the frequency of behaviors we like, such as sitting, lying down calmly, being petted, walking on a loose leash, being quiet in their crate, and so on, those behaviors are going to increase in frequency because that is how reinforcement works. And the side benefit is that, because the dog has only twenty-four hours of behavior in a day, that is going to decrease other behaviors.

The more time your dog spends doing behaviors that you like, the less time they have left over to do the things you wish they wouldn't, which means that you can sometimes essentially eclipse an unwanted behavior by rewarding the things you like so heavily that the other behavior seems unsatisfying or boring by comparison.

For example, if begging at the table has a 1% chance of producing food but lying down on a mat across the room has a 10% chance of producing food, well, dogs aren't dumb. They're going to lie on the mat. Which means that you can reduce the begging behavior in the context of meals just by providing an alternate behavior and reinforcing it heavily enough that it would be inefficient for the dog to keep doing the behavior you'd like to see less of.

What Types of Behaviors to Capture

Because capturing boils down to "Wait for the dog to do something you like and then make it pay off for them," it does have some limitations regarding the types of behaviors it can be used on.

Have you spotted the limitation?

For you to be able to pay for a behavior that your dog is already initiating on their own, the dog has to already do it some of the time. It doesn't need to be a lot of the time—you can take the tiniest spark of behavior and fan it into a bonfire with this method. But unlike our other methods of getting behavior, the spark needs to already be there in some form for you to start.

Fortunately, most of the behaviors that fall under the category of typical pet obedience are behaviors that your dog is going to offer naturally some of the time. Even the most hyper dog in the world is eventually going to stand with all four feet stationary, sit, lie down, relax onto their side and sleep. It may be for a vanishingly brief period of time, a precious second of calm in a sea of high-octane behavior, but it's there. Start with that spark and nurse it into a whole new outlook on the world.

Capturing works best with naturally-offered behaviors that are never going to be obnoxious or disruptive. For example, I don't think I've ever heard a client complain that their darn dog is sitting around calmly too much and it's cramping their style. Sits, downs, settles, lying on a bed, backing up to yield personal space, walking on a loose leash, standing on a loose leash, making eye contact and choosing to check in (like a come when called, minus the call) are all excellent behaviors to capture because they are pretty much never going to be nuisance behaviors—it's perfectly acceptable for the dog to take the initiative and offer those behaviors as much as they'd like without being told what to do.

On the flip side, be cautious about capturing any behavior that could become disruptive or pushy. My litmus test for this is, "Would it make a teenager say 'Cool'?" If so, probably not a great candidate for capturing.

While you absolutely can put captured behaviors on cue so that they're only happening when prompted, I think that loses a lot of the power of capturing and I generally don't unless I need to for some other reason. I like to use capturing to manipulate the odds of the behaviors the dog is going to naturally offer me. If I want to see more of a certain behavior, I make it pay off. If I want to see less of a different behavior, I prevent it from paying off and make something else in the same context pay off drastically better.

Building a Default Sit

If you're like most of my students, your dog already knows how to sit on cue. Some of you may even have it on a hand sign cue already—nice work! But even if your dog already knows this behavior, I want you to

CAPTURING: DEFAULT SIT

practice this exercise anyway so you can see how capturing works in real life and how it can be used to build strong default behaviors.

Put some non-perishable treats in your treat pouch and go about your daily life. But today, you are on a secret mission! Your goal is to click the moment that your dog chooses to sit down. You can pay for a dog who is already sitting too, but ideally, we're looking for the moment when the butt first hits the ground (just like clicking the tennis ball bounce earlier, but now it's your dog's butt).

They don't need to stay sitting and it's perfectly okay (and normal) if they stand up as soon as you give them the treat. That's fine.

Now go back to your daily life and keep working on whatever you were doing before you saw your dog start to initiate a sit. If they pester you for more intaction or food, disengage and ignore them without letting them access your treats. Getting one treat doesn't mean that a training session is about to start—it was just a "drive by" treat where something wonderful happened to your dog and then the interaction was over.

The first few times, it's normal for them to look a little confused. "Hey, are we doing training or not?" That's fine. Go on with your life as normal and don't be tempted to give extra cookies.

But the very next time they happen to sit, click and treat again.

This is similar to what we were doing with the eye contact game before, but it requires a bigger chunk of behavior for the same type of pay. If they're offering you the eye contact here, feel free to praise it and engage with them in a limited fashion, but our goal is more sitting and often the dogs are more likely to do that in the beginning if you ignore them just a little bit—not a full cold-shoulder, but an absent-minded half attention, like you're playing a game on your phone and peripherally aware that you have a dog but not really here to interact right now.

Over the course of the day, I want you to notice how often your dog is choosing to sit and how often you were able to catch that sit when it first began. Over the course of the next few days, keep an eye on that frequency. Is it increasing? Is your dog starting to choose to sit more often and in more contexts in hopes of a click?

As a side note, sometimes clients will send me a distress email that their dog is too smart for this game and is now gleefully manipulating them by sitting like *an absolute fiend* because they have figured out what works and they're determined to empty that treat pouch one sit at a time.

Great! What a wonderful problem to have!

If you start to feel like your dog is manipulating you by sitting all the time just to get more treats, that means you're both on the right track. The better sitting works, the less tempted they will be to choose other behaviors to try to get your attention. What a polite way for them to request what they want!

When it starts to feel "spammy," you can start to use your own discretion for which ones you pay and which ones you don't. If you like it or if it seemed polite, pay for it if you can. If it was irritating or not at a good time, don't. If you decide that you're done paying for a while, you can say "All done!" and just stop paying for any sits after that. Your dog will learn that "All done!" is a signal that reinforcement is no longer available and within a few training sessions, they'll stop offering the behavior after you've ended the session.

Luring: Spin

What Is Luring?

The next method of training we're going to learn about is called luring. You can think of a lure as a sort of treat magnet. You move the treat through space, the dog's face follows the path of the treat and the rest of the dog follows the face. Over time, this accumulates into muscle memory and the dog is able to do the full movement smoothly, and over time, you gradually prompt less and less until the dog is doing all of the steering and the treat is out of the picture.

For example, to lure a sit, pinch a treat between your thumb and first two fingers so that your dog can't chomp it loose, then magnet that treat to your dog's nose. Slowly and smoothly move the treat from the dog's nose up to their forehead, as if you wanted to paint a line on the top of their face using treat-juice. Most dogs will automatically point their nose up to try to follow the "slowly escaping" treat—as their head goes up, the butt goes down like a teeter-totter and tada, you have a sit. As soon as the butt hits the ground, give your dog the treat they were following.

Luring is easily mistaken for bribery—and in the beginning, it absolutely *is* bribery, but it develops into something much more powerful over time.

If you feel a little iffy about showing your dog the cookie before the behavior, you have good training instincts and we're going to address that in the next chapter, so stick with me. It's important that we get the lure out of the picture in the long term so the dog doesn't become dependent on a promise of rewards to do *anything*. But crucially, that doesn't mean that we can't use it in the short term—it just means we need an exit plan for it, which we'll build in the next chapter.

Benefits of Luring

The major benefit to luring is that it's downright easy and it requires very little patience on the part of the person or the dog. If you've got a few pieces of treats and a dog to work with, you can typically get behavior started in about thirty seconds, give or take.

Luring is super beginner-friendly—my friend's five-year-old kid is excellent at it, to give you an idea of how beginner-friendly it can be. The physical mechanics can feel a little wobbly the first few times you lure a specific behavior, but people tend to become proficient at luring very quickly.

For most dogs, luring comes naturally or close to it. "Move closer to food" is the absolute first thing that your dog likely learned as a newborn infant when they were blind and deaf and looking for their mother for their first meal, so it tends to come preloaded in most dogs to greater or lesser degrees—if it didn't, they would have starved to death by now. And especially if you've got a particularly desirable treat (which you should, because great treats build great behaviors), your dog is likely to be pretty motivated to move their mouth closer to that food.

And unlike the capturing we did in the previous chapter, luring requires very little patience and you get to actually *do* something to start the behavior, which is a big comfort for a lot of my students who want to be in the driver's seat with their dog's behavior. With luring, you're able to both (mostly) predict and (mostly) control the dog's eventual movement by where you put the lure, which means you don't need to trust the process as much as you do with the more hands-off methods.

In my opinion, luring is also the easiest method to attach cues to, because unlike with the other methods, you are the one in control of when the behavior is initiated even before there's an intentional command. And as a bonus, luring often tends to build a sign language cue for free in the process, so you get two cues for the price of one behavior.

Downfalls of Luring

But those benefits come with a price. The downfalls of luring tend to creep up on you over time instead of being obvious from day one, so it's easy to dismiss them as minor, but they're still worth talking about.

First, luring is more passive for the dog—which is a benefit, but also a drawback. If 90% of the dog's focus is on figuring out how to get the cheese into their face, that means that only 10% of their focus is on what they're actually doing, and that 10% is also the part whose job it is to *remember* what behavior unlocked the cheese. Luring relies less on active thinking and problem-solving and relies more heavily on muscle memory, which means that it often takes more repetition to get the behavior going independently because the dog doesn't have enough attention to focus on both the treat and what they're doing to achieve it.

And second, the line between luring and bribery is blurry and it's very important to stay on the correct side. We're going to use lures to get behaviors started, but it's not a place where you want to get stuck long term unless you want to pull a cookie out of your pocket every time you ask the dog to sit.

We use luring to *install* behaviors, but that's a very different thing from using luring to *maintain* behaviors.

Any time you use luring, have an eye on your exit plan. We're going to get the cookie out of your hand ASAP so that doesn't become a requirement for the behavior. This is about building muscle memory to get the behavior started, not long-term bribery.

Third, luring has less capacity for building precision than some of the more complex training methods and tends to work best with more general movements where you don't need a lot of fine-tuning. This isn't an issue for most pet-level training, but it's worth mentioning if you have goals of competition obedience, therapy dog work or other continuing education for your dog.

So there's a sort of trade-off with luring. On the one hand, it jumpstarts the behavior and gets things moving faster. On the other hand, it's easy to get stuck in a situation where the dog doesn't initiate the behavior *unless* you lure, which is when you start moving in the direction of bribery, which we obviously don't want to happen.

Luring a Spin in Both Directions

The first behavior we're going to lure is a spin.

I chose this behavior for two reasons:

1. Spin tends to be pretty easy to lure. The most common errors with it are things that you'll want to learn early in the luring process so you don't make the same mistakes later with behaviors you care more about.

2. It's a fun, no-pressure behavior that gives you some room to experiment without worrying that you're going to break a behavior that

you'll need to use later. Feel free to make messes and learn things with this skill.

First, pick a direction: clockwise or counter-clockwise. I am right handed and I find it easiest to lure dogs into counter-clockwise spins, but your mileage may vary and we're going to teach it in both directions in a few minutes (but one direction at a time).

Facing your dog, put a small treat into your fingers, pinched so that your dog can't chomp it, and apply that treat to your dog's nose. They should show interest in your hand. When they start trying to take the treat from your hand, gradually move your arm out to the side and around as if you wanted to slowly (slowly!) take the treat from your dog's nose and feed it to their hip instead. Your arm motion should look sort of like stirring a large pot.

Your dog's face should follow the treat because "HEY, that was my cheese! Come back!" If your dog disengages from the treat and turns away from your treat hand, re-stick the magnet back on their nose and try again, moving more slowly—I usually see this error when people are accidentally moving faster than their dog. You may also be holding your wrist too stiffly and need to rotate it a little.

A dog's spine can't bend forever (although I have certainly seen odd sleeping positions that make me question that belief), so if their mouth is moving toward their hip to take the treat, most dogs will take a step with their rear legs to straighten out their back. The second that they take a step with the rear legs, click and release the treat into their mouth.

Repeat this a few times until the movement feels fluid. As soon as the dog's legs un-stick to follow the treat, click and give it to them. You are basically taking your straight-shaped dog and "bending" them into a crescent shape as the nose tries to follow the treat to the hip.

Some dogs will jump ahead several steps and smoothly spin in a circle. Great! Pay them and keep going!

But plenty of dogs need a little more support to get moving in the beginning and they will get *much* smoother and faster with a few repetitions to practice. Keep applying the treat to the nose, moving it toward the hip and clicking for the back feet moving to straighten out the dog until that step feels pretty easy for you and your dog.

Once you have that foundation, start asking the dog to take a few more steps into the circle—not just moving the back feet a little (usually a half circle for the nose), but starting to make more of a circle (past the midpoint, more like a three-quarters turn). When you get a few of those, try for a full circle.

Once you have a full circle, practice until that feels smooth and your dog can easily follow the lure in a tight loop and end up right where he started before getting the treat.

Congratulations! You lured your first behavior! Take a well-deserved break and play with your dog.

Then in your next training session, re-teach the same behavior in the opposite direction.

For some dogs, this will require you to change luring hands, and for some you'll be able to use the same hand at a different angle. (This depends on how large your dog is and how much their spine resembles a slinky.) When switching sides, it's important that you go back to the very beginning with this step and start over from scratch—the progress that you made on turning counterclockwise does not directly help when you're turning clockwise now, so go back to baby-beginner steps and build up from there.

Even though you're starting from scratch for the new direction, you'll probably find that it's often much faster to build the second behavior than the first, and faster to build the third behavior than the second, and so on—which is why we started with a behavior that you don't need long-term (although it's a cute trick). There's often a sort of "learning how to learn" effect.

When your dog is able to smoothly follow a lure in a full circle in both directions, move on to the next step: luring a down.

Luring a Down

The next behavior that we're going to teach is a lured down.

A note: when I am teaching my own dogs, down is one of the behaviors that I end up teaching multiple ways—I typically lure it in the beginning and then switch to quite a lot of capturing. Feel free to do both and to switch between the two.

In your average puppy class, the first skill that the dog learns is a sit and the second is a down, so it is very common to see people teach a down exclusively from a sit. This is a pet peeve of mine because your dog is perfectly capable of lying down from a stand. In my opinion, it's much more practical to teach the skill from what is likely to be the starting behavior in the long term (a stand) than from an intermediate step that you don't want to get stuck with forever (a sit).

So we're going to lure a down from both a sit and a stand, because I aim to over-deliver.

Get two treats in your hand. If your dog already has a sit on cue, ask them to sit and give them the first treat for sitting. Hold the second treat between your fingers and apply to their nose, magnet-style, while they are still sitting. When the dog starts trying to take the treat from your fingers, gradually move the treat straight down toward the ground, usually aiming for the area right between your dog's front paws.

The second you see your dog's elbow start to bend, click and give them the treat. It doesn't matter if they went all the way down or just crouched a bit. The important thing is that elbow bend—once we get the elbow bend looking smooth, the rest of the down is nearly inevitable.

Your dog will probably stand up to eat their cookie and that's fine.

Reset your dog into a sit, give them their sit cookie and lure downward again, clicking again for the moment that the elbow bends. Often the dog will bend their front half a little deeper the second time—great!

If your dog is craning their neck downward like a vulture and not bending their elbows a bit, stick with it and hold out for even the tiniest bit of elbow bend. Sometimes moving the lure slightly forward or slightly backward (toward or away from the dog's chest) can unstick a stuck dog when learning this skill, so experiment a bit with that.

If your dog is coming off the lure and going back to a sit, you're almost certainly luring too quickly or too jerkily. Slow down a bit and make sure that your dog is really committed to the lure before you start moving it around. They'll gain speed as they gain confidence, so don't be afraid to go slow if that's where your dog's current skill level is.

After a few repetitions of this, start pushing the envelope on how much of an elbow bend your dog will sell you. Ask for a little bit more of a bend, and then a little bit more on the next repetition, until your dog's elbows finally hit the floor. Tada! Puppy's first down!

Repeat this process until your dog is able to go smoothly from a sit into a down as soon as you start moving the treat downward.

Once this is smooth, re-teach the same skill starting from a stand. It's often helpful to move the treat on a very slight diagonal toward the dog instead of straight down when luring a down from a stand, as if you were thinking about possibly feeding the treat to the front of their chest. This often encourages the dog to shift their weight onto their rear legs and lean backward from you so they can keep their eyes on the treat, which builds into a down the same way the bent elbows earlier in this section did.

If you're working with a very small breed dog or a dog with a very thin coat, this is often much easier to teach on a soft surface such as carpet instead of a hard surface like tile. If you have a smaller dog or a very short coated dog, practice on a soft surface until the behavior is smooth, then reteach on a hard surface afterward.

Fading a Lure: Down

Fading a Lure Quickly and Smoothly

Hooray! Now your dog is smoothly going from a sit or a stand into a down with a treat lure.

That's awesome! And it also means that it is time to move on to the next step as soon as possible so you don't get stuck with that cookie in your hand forever.

The next thing we're going to talk about is what's called "fading the lure."

It's exactly what it sounds like: making the lure itself less and less relevant to the dog's behavior so you can gradually remove the lure from the finished product.

Think of it like gradually raising the training wheels on a bike as a kid learns how to balance on their own. In the beginning, the training wheels are helpful to keep the bike upright and the kid moving in the right direction, but no one wants to be a 30-year-old who shows up to the triathlon with training wheels on their racing bike, you know?

The goal is to systematically and slowly wean the dog off the lure so that what began as a (sanctioned) bribe evolves into a hand-sign cue.

Start off by luring the behavior a few times in a row to get your dog warmed up and moving smoothly. I like to do it three or four times just to make sure there aren't any bugs in the system that I didn't catch in the last training session. If your dog struggles or seems "sticky" as you lure them down, go back to the previous step and practice more luring to get the behavior fluid and easy. If they're doing this like a pro, we're ready to move on.

On the next repetition, reach into your treat pouch as if you were getting out a treat like normal, but fake the treat. Your fingers should be pinched in the same position as usual and you should still reach into the treat pouch between reps, but nothing is actually in the hand. Really sell the process of getting the fake treat out of the pouch—use those acting skills! Quickly put the lure hand at your dog's mouth and lure downward as normal.

If you've done your homework, your dog will quickly lure into a down and most of them realize about halfway down that wait a second, that hand didn't smell like a treat at all. As soon as their elbows touch the floor, click and *immediately give them a treat from the treat pouch.*

This is important: you're fading the lure *before* the behavior, but the dog still earns the treat *after* the behavior, even if you faked them out!

If you want this behavior to be strong in the long term, the absolute worst thing you could do would be to start cheaping out on your dog at the same time as fading the lure. At this stage, if your dog does what you asked, you need to pay up.

On the next repetition, get a real treat out of your pouch and lure as normal. It's not uncommon for the dog to be a little skeptical on this rep, like "Heyyy, that last one was a fake and I need you to show me the money before we go through with this." Totally normal, totally fine, that's why we switch back to a real treat for the second rep. Don't make a big production out of proving "See, this one is real!" because you want the line between fake and real treats to get blurry.

Do a couple more with the real treats until you see the suspicion fade, and then convincingly fake a treat again, being sure to pay the dog immediately after they get the behavior right whether you had the treat in your hand already or had to reach for it in the treat pouch.

At this point, you can start to ping-pong back and forth between luring and faking a lure as your dog begins to trust that even if there's no treat in your hand, they'll still get their promised reinforcer if they follow the hand as usual. Don't break your dog's faith—if you lured it, *pay for it*.

And if it seems like I'm belaboring this point, it's because I've seen too many people get a little bit greedy and start trying to fade the treats out of the picture ASAP. Instead, they invariably end up teaching their dogs that they aren't trustworthy, which makes it infinitely harder to actually decrease your food rewards in the long term (because it's just proving to the dog that if they can't see the money, it guarantees that you're not gonna pay). As counterintuitive as it may sound, paying more heavily now is going to allow you to pay less later. Don't get greedy.

As your dog gets more and more confident with the no-treat reps, gradually switch over to consistently using the fake treat while continuing to pay from your treat pouch as soon as your dog's elbows hit the floor. You want them to be totally secure in the fact that even if they don't see the treat, you can still produce something worth working for.

Lure to Hand Sign

Once you've reached the point that you are using the fake treat 100% of the time, you have killed a bunch of birds with one stone:

1. You've taught your dog to work "on credit" so that they don't have to see the reward before beginning the behavior, even with a behavior that was initially lured.

2. You've taught your dog the beginnings of a hand sign for lying

down.

3. You've taught your dog the beginnings of a more general hand sign for following an implied lure (the pinched fingers for the fake treat), which will allow you to wean off treats faster and faster with lured behaviors in the future—because following the lure-shaped hand is *also* a behavior and you're consistently reinforcing it.

But you're not done there!

Right now, you still have to lure the dog all the way down to the floor to get the down behavior, and if your back is anywhere near as old and creaky as mine (I'm thirty, when did I develop a creaky back, send help), that's getting irritating and/or painful pretty quickly. Wouldn't it be nice if you could get the dog started and then have them do the rest of the behavior on their own so you didn't have to bend over so far?

It sure would! Which is why the next step is going to be transitioning that implied lure to a hand sign, which will allow you to give the down cue without bending all the way over so you don't single-handedly fund a mansion for your chiropractor.

Get your dog warmed up with the implied lure from the previous step. Once they're doing that confidently and comfortably, start to "slur" your lure a little bit (also, if you enjoy tongue-twisters, try saying "slur your lure" ten times fast just for fun). Instead of going all the way down to the floor with the dog, maybe stop an inch above the floor. It's normal for the dog to bobble a bit on the first repetition or two, but they should get it pretty quickly—if it's been more than three repetitions and your dog still looks uncertain, you're moving too quickly.

Do make sure that your dog is still in their down when you give them the treat. You don't want them to down and then bounce back to a stand to take the cookie. You can either bend a bit on your treat delivery or use the drop-to-floor delivery that we practiced in an earlier section.

Gradually, inch by inch, start to cut corners on the lure until you're only beginning the behavior by lowering your hand a couple of inches and your dog is happily throwing themself the rest of the way to the floor without your help. Continue to pay once elbows touch the floor.

If the dog stops doing the behavior or visibly balks, go back to a much easier step and get them back on the right track, then train forward again.

Once you're able to barely lower your hand and the dog is happily flattening into a down, start to "slur" your hand sign from the lure shape to whatever you'd like the final hand sign to be. Mine is a flat palm facing downward, as if I wanted to push an invisible box down into the floor. Repeat this until your dog is smoothly lying down from a sit or a stand when you make the hand sign.

Congratulations! You have your first hand sign cue.

Side Note: Why Hand Signs Rock

Did I mention that hand signs rock? Because they do!

Dogs are typically much more attuned to body language than we are, which makes absolute sense for a non-verbal social species with a rich vocabulary of body language. We humans tend to be very focused on verbal behavior, but for dogs, body language is usually much more relevant, so it's often faster to put a new behavior on a hand sign cue than a verbal.

Plus, it's just darned convenient to be able to ask your dog to perform their behaviors without even speaking to them. Being able to ask your dog to lay down, wait there and hush while you're on the phone without interrupting your own conversation feels a little bit like magic. Fortunately, it takes very little extra effort to add on a hand sign with a behavior that you're teaching—in fact, it often takes more effort to get rid of it than to solidify it, so you may as well take the freebie cue.

Shaping: Settle on a Mat

What Is Shaping?

I know I've used the word "magical" a few times in this book already, but when it comes to training magic, shaping is the real MVP.

"Shaping by successive approximations" is a mouthful, but if you've ever played the guessing game "Warmer, Colder," you're familiar with this tool already.

Shaping is just the warmer side of "Warmer, Colder." It involves setting up the environment in such a way that the learner is likely to make the decision that you want, and then gradually sculpting their behavior in the direction of the behavior you're looking for. Behavior moving in the direction of the goal is reinforced and behavior moving away from the goal is not. The criteria change so slowly that the learner stays engaged with the process the whole time and you only gradually weed out the least successful repetitions at any stage along the way. By selecting for the behaviors moving in the right direction, the behavior gradually evolves in the direction of the reinforcement.

In other words, shaping works kind of like "survival of the fittest" for behaviors. Since behaviors which are reinforced tend to be repeated and built upon, and behaviors which are not reinforced tend to lose momentum, you can sculpt the direction the behavior evolves in.

If that sounds complicated, it can be, but it can also be much easier than people give it credit for—there are definitely easy, beginner-friendly shaping projects and we're going to go over some of them in this chapter.

Benefits of Shaping

Oh, where to even begin the list!

The major benefit of shaping is that it is almost infinitely flexible. If an animal can physically perform the behavior, you can shape them to do it.

Trainers in zoos are masters of this. If you've ever seen a hyena present their jugular vein for a voluntary blood draw, a giraffe present their foot for a pedicure, a hippo hold their mouth open so someone can brush their teeth or an orca pee in a cup (yes, really), then you've seen the power of shaping in practice. And if you haven't seen those things yet, a YouTube search for veterinary training in zoos is today's homework.

Shaping can move behavioral mountains. It is the big guns, the heavy artillery, the big kahuna.

Shaping is also a scalpel. It allows for a truly remarkable level of precision, to the point that you can micro-shape the movements of individual muscles to build extraordinarily precise, defined behaviors. It's dressage, it's ballet, it's a symphony. You know those multi-layer microscope glasses that watchmakers wear? It's that, but for behavior. You can zoom in, and zoom in, and zoom in.

But if you're not a training geek yet, that's probably not very motivating to you, because you bought this book to learn how to train your dog the basics and here I am going on about watchmakers and scalpels. Apologies!

In practical terms for a beginner audience, shaping is how you raise the difficulty level on pretty much any of the other skills that we're going to teach in this book. You can't do much training at all without shaping in some way; sometimes it's just more explicit.

Any time you're building up criteria (for example, any time you have read the word "gradually" in this book, which is probably about every third paragraph), what you're actually doing is shaping, nested inside another method—but you can do it on its own too.

Shaping is systematic improvement toward an end goal.

Downfalls of Shaping

The major downfall of shaping as a standalone method is that it's less beginner-friendly than the other exercises for the human end of the leash. An inexperienced human shaping an inexperienced dog can be frustrating, whereas with capturing and luring, there's a little more room for error.

You may have noticed that in the previous section, the examples and analogies were mostly skilled trades: dressage, ballet, symphony, watchmaker, surgeon's scalpel. And the thing that all of those have in common is that they're not entry-level jobs.

Likewise, shaping is usually presented as a more advanced type of training, and while it absolutely *can* be, I think it can also be made accessible to an entry-level audience. It may take a lot more experience to be able to shape the behavioral equivalent of the Mona Lisa, but the basics of shaping are also the fundamentals of good training in general.

The other major downfall of shaping if you spend much time in the dog training community is that a lot of people have a sort of fuzzy definition of what shaping really looks like. There was a well-known exercise called 101 Things To Do With A Box which was broadly misinterpreted in the training community, and it led to a lot of people believing that shaping is a calculus-level exercise because frankly, they were making it way harder than it needed to be.

There is a misconception in some corners of the dog training community that shaping means giving your learner as little information as possible and building the entire behavior from scratch in the "purest" possible form, starting with tiny components of behavior and not helping yourself at all with your reward placement, props or physical environment.

This is silly, and also not very good shaping.

That method is frustrating, and it's frustrating because it is fundamentally flawed. If you've tried that kind of shaping before and found it daunting, let's start in kindergarten instead of calculus and see if it's a little more approachable!

Easy Intro Shaping Games

The secret of shaping is that if you look closely enough, almost any training you do is some variety of shaping. Any time we start off with lower criteria and gradually raise the bar as our dog succeeds, we're shaping in the direction of our goals.

Starting with just an elbow bend when we were luring downs and then asking for a full down? That was shaping.

Gradually fading the lure out of the picture until we were able to lure with an empty hand? Also shaping.

Changing that lure into a hand sign that means the same thing? Yep, that was shaping too.

So you've already had a little practice with this in other contexts, but now we're going to raise the bar a little on your skills (because hey, this book is about shaping *you* too).

In the beginning, shaping looks a lot like capturing, the method we used for eye contact and sits in the earlier chapters. Just like with capturing, you're letting the dog take the initiative on the behavior. Your job is to set up the environment to make the behavior you want likely to happen and then to reinforce it strategically. The dog gets to pick all of the behaviors, but you get to stack the deck to make your preferred behaviors more likely.

What you're going to look for is the smallest unit of the end behavior, the behavioral acorn that will eventually grow into an oak tree. For example, when we were looking for a down, we started with an elbow bend. If you have a dog who is already sitting and you start encouraging them to bend their elbows more and more, a down is almost inevitable.

In general, you want the dog to be right about 80% to 90% of the time before moving on to the next step, so we're looking for the very smallest unit of behavior that will get them moving on the right track. And unlike with the human "Warmer, Colder" game, we're reinforcing each step many times before adjusting the criteria.

Or in other words, you're reinforcing almost everything that your dog offers in the direction of your chosen goal, and you're just shaving off the lowest 10% to 20% of behaviors which are the furthest away from your goal. Behavior follows reinforcement, so the trend of the behavior is going to gradually move in the direction you want it to go if you weed out the duds and pay for everything else.

It's important to note that shaping is best done quietly. It may be tempting to prompt or "help" your dog, but in most cases, verbal help is more likely to distract your dog than to help them. Our job is to set up the training situation and reinforce correctly, but the behavior itself is the dog's responsibility. Focus on your part of the relationship and let the dog handle the behavior. Giving up a little bit of control now is going to give you a lot more control in the long term.

Shaping Four Paws in a Box

For this exercise, you'll need a cardboard box at least as long and as wide as your dog, but bigger is fine. Ideally, something about chest-height on your dog is perfect, but too low is better than too tall. I've taught this with a pizza box, so it doesn't need to be anything fancy as long as your dog could stand in it comfortably.

Set the box down directly in front of you and steady it with your feet so it doesn't slide.

Be ready to click for any interest in the box as soon as you set it down. You'll usually get a look, a nose poke and moving in the direction of the box very quickly, so be ready for it—any of those behaviors are clickable.

At this stage, click any interaction with the box at all. If you ask yourself "Does X count," the answer is yes.

You can pay for pretty much any other behavior which acknowledges the continued existence of the box in their world. The bar is *so* low at this stage you could almost trip over it—they would almost have to be trying to *not* do something clickable. You should be clicking about every five seconds for most dogs. If it's much longer than that, you are probably looking for too much behavior. Be *generous* at this step! When in doubt, click it and pay.

Pretty soon, your dog should be orienting toward the box and starting to offer more targeted behavior in its direction. "What does my owner want me to do with this, then? Something about the box? How does this box make them pay me?"

In particular, pay for any time your dog's paw or leg touches the box. If you get pawing, great! If they put their foot in the box, even better!

To super-charge this skill, deliver your reward in the box itself if it's low enough for your dog to easily lean in to get the treat, or hold it directly above the box at dog-face-height if the box is too tall. By placing the reward where you want the dog to end up, you can create a subtle magnet effect that will gradually encourage your dog to move closer and closer to where the reward appears—but remember that your criterion right now is just *any* interaction with the box.

What percentage of your dog's behavior is oriented toward the box right now? If you would estimate that it's upward of 80%, start looking at which percentage of your dog's behavior is oriented toward the box using their paws in some way.

Once your dog is reliably interacting with the box with their paws, gradually reinforce for interactions with their nose or eyes less often until you're not paying for them at all. Only paw behaviors count, but *any* paw behaviors toward the box count.

Eventually, they're going to land a paw in the box. When this happens, click and pay repeatedly rapidfire in the box for as long as one paw is in there, up to about ten treats in a row. Then toss one treat off to the side to reset your dog for the next repetition.

The reset allows them to offer the same behavior again from the beginning. In other words, you can think of "go to the box" and "stay in the box" as different behaviors and we want them to practice both halves, so they've gotta leave the box so they can practice getting back to it.

Go back to paying for any pawing. We've gotten one repetition of a paw in the box, but that doesn't pass the 80% test, so your dog isn't ready to move on yet. If another paw lands in the box, pay rapidfire for as long as the paw is in the box and reset again.

After a few repetitions of this, most dogs will start to step into the box with one front paw or both front paws and it will start to look a lot more deliberate. If you get one treat for touching the box with your paw and ten treats for putting your paw inside the box, most dogs are going to pick the ten treats. Pay multiple treats in a row when they get the paw in the box, then toss a treat to reset.

Once your dog figures out the goal, it's common for them to make a small leap ahead. "If putting one paw in the box is great, putting two paws in the box must be even better!" When they start offering that behavior consistently, you can stop rewarding one paw in the box and hold out for both front paws in the box.

And after they've offered front paws in the box repeatedly and with confidence, start looking for that third paw and gradually taper off paying for two paws.

Then the fourth paw.

Have fun with this step! Now you have a dog hoping into and out of a box for fun and you never had to say a word to make it happen: you just took care of the consequences and the dog took care of the behavior.

Where can you use this skill? Well, yesterday I used a variation on exactly this setup to convince a 60-pound German Shepherd/Belgian Malinois mix that she could fit into the footwell of a very cramped car because she needed to ride with us and there was no space in the back seat. I shaped her to sit in the footwell exactly the same way I had shaped her to jump in the box as a puppy, except it only took about a minute with the much-more-challenging car because she already had practice with thinking like this. You can use a similar method to teach a dog to go into their crate, stand on the scale at the vet, get into the bathtub or pose with a prop for a photoshoot.

This is just the barest tip of the iceberg for shaping! And each new behavior you shape is going to make the next one go a little bit faster.

Shaping Go to Mat

Our next shaping project is going to be teaching your dog to settle on a mat. This is a fantastically helpful behavior for all sorts of things and one of the very first behaviors I teach to any dog who comes into my household.

As we mentioned in a previous chapter, dogs are great at learning specifics and significantly less great at learning general concepts. Teaching a dog the abstract concept of a stay takes some work. Teaching a dog "if you see a mat, you should be lying down calmly on it" is much easier because it's much more specific. It gives the dog very clear criteria for what correct looks like and exactly where the boundaries are, whereas stays can be muddy (e.g., how slumpy can a sit-stay get and still be a sit?).

I like to use a raised surface of some sort for this. My favorites are the cot-style dog beds (called hammocks in some areas) because the raised surface seems to help the dogs get the idea faster, but anything with a different surface from the regular floor will work and if you're able to use something slightly raised, that will help. A regular dog bed, sofa cushion or bath mat will work just fine.

Start off with a handful of treats and position the mat between you and a wall, leaving a foot or two on either side of the mat if possible for the dog to move. You're basically making a very short hallway with your body as a wall.

Toss a treat onto the mat to get the behavior started—technically a lure, but we're only using the one.

Your dog will step onto the mat to get the treat. The second their foot touches the mat, click again and toss the next treat about a foot away from the mat in the direction they were already facing. You don't want the dog to have to search for the dropped treat, but you do want them to have to leave the mat to get it, so about a foot is good for most dogs.

Continue to stand in front of the mat, facing the mat.

Most dogs will turn to look at you to figure out why you're looking at a wall, why you're throwing treats and where the next one is going to land. Click the first step as they turn back toward you (and the mat!) and toss the treat off to the other side of the mat so they walk across the mat to get to it.

If they happen to step onto the mat in the process of figuring out whether you're likely to pay again, immediately click, drop one treat on the mat and toss another about a foot away. So they get one treat for turning or double treats for stepping on the mat.

After a few repetitions, raise the bar. Now they have to touch one paw to the mat before you click and toss the treat off the mat ahead of them. You should always be throwing the treat in the direction that the dog is moving already. If you remember the targeting game we played in one of the earlier chapters where your dog was picking up a tossed treat, returning to the center to boop your hand and then going to get a tossed treat in the other direction, this should feel very familiar.

Repeat this step until it's looking smooth. Ideally, you want them to pick up the tossed treat and immediately orient back toward the mat, like "And I can do it *again,* too!" Your dog doesn't need to wait on the mat yet and we're just looking for *one* paw to touch the mat surface. It helps to think of the mat as a huge treat-producing button that your dog can push with his body. If any part of him touches the treat button, click and toss a treat.

Within about twenty repetitions, you should have a nice loop building up where the dog is yo-yoing onto and off of the mat in either direction. Some dogs pick it up faster, some slower, but twenty is probably a good ballpark figure. It won't look like a settle yet at all, but it should definitely look like *something* starting to take shape.

Our diagnostic for whether your dog is ready to move on to the next step is the part of the sequence where the dog eats the treat from the previous repetition and then goes back to the mat. If they swallow the treat and immediately turn back to the mat for the next repetition, you're ready for the next step. If they swallow the treat, sniff around, offer you a sit, scratch and then go, "Oh yeah! The mat!" then you're not ready to move on yet. Keep practicing at this level until the dog is almost *insisting* on being on the mat as soon as they can. The mat will take on a sort of magnetic quality.

When your dog is magneting back to the mat every time you toss a treat, raise the criteria slightly. Now you're looking for two paws on the mat before you click and treat. It doesn't need to be the front two and the dog doesn't need to be doing it on purpose, but now you're only clicking when two paws are on the mat. Continue tossing the treat about a foot off to the side.

Once your dog is consistently offering you two paws on the mat, raise the criteria to three paws the same way. Then four paws.

At this point, you have a dog who rushes back to the mat and plants with all four paws for a treat, which is the beginning of your settle. Once you've got that, the rest is easy!

Shaping a Settle on the Mat

Now we're going to change the game a little bit. Instead of tossing the treat to reward every time, we're going to pay multiple times for four paws on the mat, then toss a treat to reset, just like with the box game.

So the new sequence is going to be ten treats placed directly on the mat, rapidfire, click-treat-click-treat, for as long as all four paws are on the mat. Then click and toss the eleventh treat off the mat to the side to reset your dog.

When you're placing the ten treats, set them directly on the mat instead of tossing—ideally between your dog's front paws, but close enough is close enough. We want to minimize treat movement while they're on the mat to build a more stationary behavior and we want there to be lots of contrast with the tossed treat for the reset.

After you've done this once or twice, take a good long break, possibly for the rest of the day—at least on this skill. This is a *lot* of thinking for a novice dog and we don't want to burn them out by asking for too much too fast.

When you come back to the project, start from scratch with just one paw touching the mat, then work up from there exactly the same way as before.

It should go much faster the next time since your dog already has some experience. It's not uncommon for the dogs to skip steps. "Mom, that's puppy stuff! Look, I can already do four paws on the mat. Just feed me cheese." That's great! If they're willing to move ahead, by all means, move ahead!

When you get to the ten treats on the mat step, start off clicking and placing the treats on the mat one at a time as fast as you can go. It shouldn't take more than thirty seconds. Click-treat-click-treat.

On the next repetition, start to space out the treats just slightly—no more than a second or so between clicks, with each click followed immediately by a treat. Click-treat-pause, click-treat-pause.

If we've done our job right, your dog should stay on the mat even with the very slightly slower treat delivery. (If not, go back to an earlier step and work your way forward. You know the drill at this point.) Repeat the ten treats with all four paws on the mat with a brief pause between treats, then follow with one treat tossed off the side.

Gradually start to increase the amount of pause in between treats. When I say gradually here, I mean in units of a second at a time or less. We want the dog to think it's an absolute no-brainer to stand on this mat and wait for food.

If your dog offers you a sit or a down, or even body language that looks like they're thinking in that direction, pay like gangbusters. That's a huge step forward! Remember that for the treats on the mat, you want to be placing them directly onto the mat rather than tossing them. It's ideal if you can deliver the treat directly between the dog's front paws each time. This minimizes how much your dog moves in between treats, which is going to make it easier to build that sit or down. It's also going to get you an automatic neck-bend and possibly an elbow-bend, and we learned in the down chapter that that makes a down much more likely.

If your dog offers you a sit or a down, raise the rate of reinforcement when they are sitting or lying down so that you are paying rapidfire for sits and downs on the mat, and still paying but more slowly for standing with all four feet on the mat.

Now we're going to focus on the settle component by rewarding faster and more reliably for sits and downs, then building in small pauses while the dog is standing. Your dog is clever and if we've picked our reinforcers right, they want The Good Stuff. Their behavior is going to move in the direction that involves more food, which means you'll see less standing and more lying down, especially if you're careful with placing the treats instead of tossing them where they might bounce off the mat.

Shortly, you should have a dog who is going to the mat and immediately sitting or lying down.

The end goal is to have a dog who can automatically gravitate toward the mat from a foot or two away, then automatically lie down on the mat and wait for three or four seconds between treats for a total of about ten treats. Once you have that, let's move on!

This is the beginning of an automatic settle on a mat. We'll come back to this skill in a later section when we teach stays. For now, feel free to leave the mat available (if your dog is unlikely to chew it) and add down on a mat to the list of behaviors that you can capture if you happen to catch them making the right choice on their own, along with sit and eye contact. A "mat addict" is a wonderful thing to have.

Attaching a Cue: Potty

Yay, You Finally Get to Talk!

In this section, we're going to start attaching cues, which means that yay, you finally get to talk!

First, though, let's talk about why I've asked you to do the previous exercises *without* talking to your dog, because that's important. There are several reasons, but the primary ones are:

1. It would have distracted your dog when they were building their framework for training, which would have slowed down their learning.
2. Your dog doesn't need it.
3. I wanted you to *see* that your dog doesn't need it so you would trust that the power is in the consequences, not in the magic words.

Culturally, it makes sense to us that the power in dog training comes from the command. That's what makes the dog do the thing, right?

Nope! What makes the dog do the thing is their learning history, and their learning history starts with the consequences. It is entirely possible to teach a dog a wide variety of skills without ever saying a word, because as far as the dog is concerned, consequence is king.

In fact, when you think about it, it's kind of ridiculous how much focus we put on the words. Animals learn to behave for consequences *constantly* in nature. The ability to learn from the consequences they encounter is literally what keeps them alive every day in the wild. Only a teeny tiny fraction of those animals have humans involved in their care at all due to domestication, and an even smaller fraction of those animals are taught verbal cues for specific behaviors.

Dogs spoil us by humoring our need to use words constantly (one of the many ways in which they are wonderful), but the words are generally for our benefit, not theirs.

If it pays off, the dog will keep doing it. If it doesn't pay off, the dog will stop doing it. It can be as simple as that.

Okay, so if it's that simple, why are we talking *now?*

Because sometimes it would be convenient to be able to ask for a specific behavior that you've already taught so your dog knows which behavior earns them the consequence they want. The cue lets them take a shortcut straight to the right action instead of flipping through their rolodex of potentially reinforcing behaviors (at least half of which were installed by mother nature, such as "chew on it" or "pee on it" and so on).

In other words, cues don't force the behavior to happen—they just tell the dog which set of consequences is in play at any given time. Likewise, a green light doesn't force your car to move forward, but it tells you that foot-on-gas-pedal will be reinforced now (with forward progress) instead of punished (with a potential ticket or wreck).

How Cues Work

Cues are functionally the labels that tell your learner which behaviors are likely to pay off right now.

I like to think of them as the bookie at a horse race or something like that. "Hey Mike, hot tip: it sounds like we've got a bidder for a sit real soon."

Cues save your dog a phenomenal amount of effort. Imagine if dogs spent all day trying to figure out when rolling over was worth doing and when it wasn't. Wouldn't it be handy to be able to tell them, "By the way, I'm only paying if I've said the words 'roll over,' and if you do it on your own at any other time, that's volunteer work." Seems like it would save them a lot of guessing!

So just to reiterate, the cues don't inherently force the behavior to happen and there is nothing magical about:

1. What word you say
2. How you say it
3. What tone of voice you use
4. What language you speak it in

Or anything else in that vein.

These things don't matter because the point of the cue is its relationship to the behavior and the consequence. A cue with no behavior and no consequence attached is meaningless noise.

And for that matter, most of the cues in your dog's life aren't even verbal.

Have you ever seen a dog race to the door as soon as you touch the leash? That's a cue.

Or come running when you crinkle the treat bag? Also a cue.

Or hop up on the sofa when you pat the cushion? Cue.

Or leap up to greet you when you walk through the door? Cue.

Or eat when you put the food bowl down? Cue.

Or bark at the mailman? Cue.

Who knew that your dog knew so many cues! (Now there's a tongue-twister.)

"But that's different!" you protest, "I'm talking about the *commands* that we use in training. That's a whole different category of thing!"

You're right, but you're mostly wrong. Let's talk about it!

The Difference Between Cues and Commands

You're right to feel that there's a significant difference between a cue and a command, but if you're like most of my training clients, you're wrong about what that difference is.

A cue is a signal that reinforcement may be available for a specific behavior. It's a green light to do the thing that you already want to do because you know it pays off.

A command is a signal that you have the opportunity to avoid something unpleasant and if you don't get it right, something bad will happen to you. A command is a warning bell that you had better do the right thing at the right time or else.

That's not just semantics and the distinction is crucial to dog training.

In modern dog training based on positive reinforcement, we use cues, which means that we're giving the dog a hint at which behaviors will pay off for dogs. We do not use commands, which are threats that if the dog does not perform the correct behavior, they will be punished. And the line between the two is black and white.

If you treat your cues like commands, they will break. They will break because you will be breaking your promise that something good may be coming after the cue. If you give a positively taught cue and then punish the dog for not complying, the line between a cue and a command degrades and so does the reliability of your behavior.

Cues require you to work on the assumption that your dog wants to do the thing that you're going to ask them to do, or that they have any reason to believe that would work out well for them. If you mix in a layer of *or else*, you risk contaminating that, which trainers call creating a "poisoned cue." Poisoned cues are about as unpleasant as the name makes them sound, so you want to avoid poisoning your cues as much as possible—which means keeping the cue's association with reinforcement as uncontaminated by punishment as possible.

And that "or else" can be tempting because it comes with the illusion of control. If you don't know better, it looks a lot like a safety net.

But contrary to what you may expect, a positively-trained cue is *at least* as powerful as a punishment-trained command if taught correctly, and the positively-trained cue can become even more powerful with time and repetition. Because in reality, that tempting "or else" contingency is not as solid as it looks. It's more of a safety blanket than a safety net, by which I mean that it is more about *feeling* secure than *being* secure.

For example, raise your hand if you have ever had to give a command multiple times to get your dog to listen or grumbled that your dog is just so *stubborn* that he needs constant reminders to stay in line. That's not a problem with boundaries and it's not because your dog is extra-difficult. It's the hidden cost of teaching commands instead of cues.

In other words, if your training method boils down to "I can *make* you do it," you're signing up for a lot more "Oh yeah? Then try to make me, bro" than necessary. You can get solid results without getting into a battle of wills with your dog.

That's part of why I chose toileting as the first behavior you get to attach a cue to. Most of us have grown up in a world full of "or else" contingencies and it takes some practice to adjust that mindset. Short of literally scaring the poop out of them, it is darned difficult to "or else" a dog into going potty—the more you bluster at them, the less likely they are to go. Your options are on-cue or off-cue, but you're not going to get it on-command.

And once you have practice with teaching cues, you can build them up to extreme reliability. The more often you pair cue -> behavior -> reward, the tighter that loop gets and the more automatic the response becomes.

For example, when you were learning to drive, you learned "green light means go" as a cue rather than a command. Your reinforcement was forward progress toward wherever you were driving to. Barring the occasional horn toot from a car behind you, there is not much of an "or else" to force you to drive when a light turns green—but I can still guarantee that if you've been a driver for a while, your foot almost automatically moves to the gas pedal when you see a green light. Why? Because cues can be *incredibly powerful* with repeated practice and reinforcement—no "or else" required.

Attaching the Cue

So let's talk about how to build cues into your training.

To attach a cue, the first step is to get the behavior happening reliably at a time that you can predict. The behavior should already be happening consistently before you start putting the cue on, otherwise the dog will have no idea what that word is supposed to be attached to and you won't get very far. As far as your dog is concerned, it will just be a random unit of gibberish hanging in the air, no different than any of the other verbal flotsam that we humans throw about with such enthusiasm. Your dog will tune it out.

For this exercise, we're going to use pottying on cue. I picked this behavior because most people haven't already taught it, almost everyone can benefit from it and it's extremely unlikely that you would be able to accidentally use a command-based method to attach a cue to pottying (short of squeezing the pee right out of them, which I very much hope you will not attempt and I obviously would not endorse).

This book is meant to be a teach-a-man-to-fish book, which means that I want you to leave with the ability to attach a cue to anything, including behaviors that your dog offers without your assistance. If you can attach a cue to peeing, you can attach a cue to anything by the same method. If you're an overachiever and you've already attached

ATTACHING A CUE: POTTY

cues to some of the behaviors we taught earlier in the book, you may already be a pro at this, but it's likely that this will be more challenging because you can't directly prompt the behavior another way.

Ready?

We're going to begin by cheating.

Pick a time when your dog is very likely to need to go to the bathroom already. This is called **antecedent arrangement**, which means you're setting up your learner to do the thing that you want to reinforce, or otherwise making it more likely that the behavior will occur.

Bring some treats with you even if you don't usually pay for potty and take the dog outside as normal, whether that means on leash or in the yard.

Partially ignore your dog. Keep an eye on them, but don't drill holes into them with your eyes; you'll creep them out and creeped out dogs don't pee.

The second when you decide your dog is definitely about to pee, say your potty cue. Ours is "go potty" at my house because I am very original, but yours can be whatever you'd like as long as it's consistent.

Ideally, you want to say the cue precisely at the point of no return: when they've just barely committed to the behavior but it would take more work to *not* do it than to follow through. In practice, that's usually about one second before you think they're actually going to do whatever you're trying to put on cue for most behaviors.

If your dog went potty right after the cue, hooray! Pay your dog as soon as they finish! (NOT once you get back inside. That's unlikely to reinforce anything except coming through the door.)

In this case, pottying is naturally a slightly reinforcing behavior because it relieves an overly full bladder, but it never hurts to be generous and put a treat on the behavior too. And as an aside, one of my personal pet peeves is waiting forever-and-a-day for a dog to go potty, so I would much rather pay a couple pieces of kibble a day per dog to never have to stand in the rain waiting for my dog to find the perfect blade of grass to bless again, but your mileage may vary on that.

So, does your dog know what "go potty" means now?

Not a bit. That was one repetition.

How many repetitions it takes to attach a cue varies dramatically from dog to dog, but somewhere between fifty and a hundred repetitions seems to be average, with a broad range of outliers in both directions.

Practice this every time you take your dog outside for a week or two and I guarantee two things:

1. You'll have a much better understanding of how cues work, and

2. Your dog will begin to understand how to potty promptly when asked.

Troubleshooting Cues

Okay, now let's talk about what can go wrong with attaching a cue.

The most common thing is that you think your dog is about to do the behavior, you add the cue before it, and... nothing. They don't do it. Sometimes they even look at you in confusion like "Why would you interrupt me like this? I was about to do the thing."

Ouch. Sorry, friend! It happens to the best of us.

So, what do you do about it?

Nothing, mostly. It's going to happen once in a while and it's no big deal if it's occasional.

If it's happening repeatedly when you're attaching the cue, you may be giving the cue too early or you may be working with a particularly sensitive dog who is easily intimidated by feeling like they're in the spotlight. Try delaying an extra second or two until the dog has actually started to do the behavior, then label it while they're doing it and reinforce. This doesn't do much to actually build the cue itself, so

ATTACHING A CUE: POTTY

you're going to have to gradually move the cue earlier in the process, but it can give you a place to start with a dog who routinely balks every time you try to put a cue on a behavior.

Much less frequently, I see a dog who hears the cue, does the behavior, gets the treat, and then starts "spamming" their owner with the same behavior over and over and over in hopes of additional treats, which is a harmless waste of energy that will resolve on its own if you don't pay for it in the majority of cases. "I sit, I sit again, I sit yet again, did you want to pay for this one, what about this one, I can sit even more times than this, you just tell me when to stop, how many sits does it take to get a cookie around here?"

The solution to this is what trainers call building **stimulus control**. Stimulus control means that the behavior happens when you ask for it and doesn't happen when you don't ask for it because the dog knows it won't pay off. There's some technical stuff too, but that's the important part. So when you're teaching a dog that the presence of a cue is a green light that the behavior will be reinforced, you are also teaching them that the behavior will *not* be reinforced unless it's cued in some way.

Note that not every behavior needs to be on stimulus control. Far from it! I keep a wide range of behaviors off stimulus control because I want my dogs to be able to independently offer them when they make sense. For example, I teach my dogs to go to their mats and lie down when cued, but I also frequently reinforce them for making that decision on their own without any input from me because I can't remember the last time I was frustrated that my dog was lying down calmly *too* much. Know what I mean?

But for behaviors which can be dangerous, damaging, intrusive, noisy, obnoxious or inconvenient, stimulus control is important. Make sure the dog has plenty of opportunities to do the behavior on cue and get reinforced for it, and then stop paying the voluntary versions that you didn't ask for.

Ever taught a dog to shake and then gotten enthusiastically paw-whacked every time they think you might have a treat? Stimulus control fixes that.

And again, I don't do this with polite household behaviors and I don't recommend that you do either. So for example, I would never put sit on total stimulus control because I want my dogs to offer sit as their default guess when they're not sure what behavior unlocks The Good Stuff. My dogs are free to spam me with voluntary sits as often as they want and I'll decide whether or not I feel like paying in that context. But I would absolutely put shake paws on stimulus control ASAP because I have no desire to be whacked by a big old German Shepherd paw every fifteen minutes in case I decide to be generous and share a cookie.

"Okay, so when do I get to say the cue whenever I want and get that behavior?"

Short version: when you've earned it.

In the beginning, don't test your cue against distractions yet. We're getting there later in the book, but we're not there now and you're just going to break your cues if you ask the dog for behaviors in situations when you're pretty sure they're not going to make the right decision. Even if your dog is a champion of sitting in the living room, don't use the cue yet in the middle of the dog park when they're playing a noisy game of chase with their buddies—you haven't leveled it up enough for that yet.

We're going to systematically teach your dog to ignore distractions and respond to your cues even when cool stuff is going on in the environment, but that is not a "day one, step one" project.

The rule of thumb when you're thinking about using a new cue is to ask yourself whether you'd be willing to bet someone $20 that your dog will do the behavior on the first try after only being asked once. If you feel a little squeamish about making that bet, you're probably not ready to use the cue in that situation yet.

ATTACHING A CUE: POTTY

There's no shame in that! It's better to keep a cue as solid as possible and avoid using it when you're just gambling, because every time you give the cue and it *doesn't* end in reinforcement for your dog, you're also taking some of the power out of that cue in the long run and teaching your dog that it's not relevant. It's basically dinging your credit score with your dog.

And please, I beg you: Say the cue once. Not three times. If you find yourself chanting your cue at your dog, "Sit, sit, *sit, siiiit,*" that's a giant neon sign that says you're using the cue too early or in an environment that you haven't earned yet.

Zip it! If saying the cue once isn't enough, then that's your diagnostic that something is wrong. Saying it six more times does not fix the problem.

If your dog doesn't respond, it's important to remember that your dog isn't "just being stubborn." Stubborn is from a command-based perspective where there's a do-it-or-else component. We're using *cues*, which means that our words are a promise of The Good Stuff, not a threat of The Bad Stuff. Even the most "stubborn" dog on the planet would have absolutely no reason to snub our cues because we're just telling them how to get more cheese in their life. And who doesn't want more cheese in their life?

3

Self-Control Behaviors

Voluntary Leave It

The Skill That Will Save Your Dog's Life

"Okay," you may be thinking, "That positive stuff is fine, but what about when my dog is going to do something dangerous? How do I teach them *not* to do something?"

That's why we're going to teach your dog to leave things alone when asked.

Leave it is often thought of as impulse control or resisting temptation on cue. Traditionally, it was taught as a warning that The Bad Stuff was going to happen if the dog approached whatever they were asked to leave. For example, I have personally seen another trainer tell a student to punch their dog in the face (and yes, she mimed a *punch*) if their dog ever approached a thing they'd been asked to leave.

So, needless to say, we will *not* be teaching it that way.

The way I teach a leave it is completely in line with the rest of the positive reinforcement philosophy in this book—and just as powerful. The fact that this skill may save your dog's life doesn't mean that you have to hurt the dog to install it. You can teach strong, reliable, fast and precise behaviors using positive reinforcement, including teaching your dog to avoid interacting with something that they would like to interact with.

Leave It = Turn Away + Eye Contact

The way I teach the skill, "leave it" is a cue that means that I would like my dog to turn their nose away from the thing that they want and make eye contact with me, because it's very hard for dogs to get into trouble with most of the things we're asking them to leave in real life while turning away and making eye contact.

Like most of positive training, this requires some re-framing if you're used to a more command-based structure where leave it was taught as a way to scold the dog for something they'd already done wrong or were about to do wrong. We're not scolding the dog for anything—we're asking for an alternative behavior and we're going to show them that our way pays off better than their way.

Besides the obvious benefits of skipping the part where you scare, hurt or intimidate your dog (and you love your dog, so why would you want to do any of that if you didn't have to?), training a leave it with positive reinforcement is much less likely to create a dog who just learns to be sneaky about their naughty behavior to avoid punishment.

Show of hands, how many readers had strict parents with strict rules? And I'm going to bet that about 80% of you rapidly learned to circumvent those rules as soon as you knew they wouldn't be backed up, because when threats are the only thing ensuring your compliance, you become *very* motivated to find blind spots in those threats. I wasn't a sneak-out-the-window sort of kid, but I definitely uninstalled the parental controls on my computer which were designed to turn it off automatically at bedtime every night.

So we're not going to be strict parents even for this lifesaving skill because being strict creates only the *illusion* of power. Good stimulus control is real power and that's how we're going to do it.

Building Impulse Control with Slow Treats

Most of the families I work with have a routine where the dog waits for their dinner bowl to be put down, and most of their routines look the same. I would say that upwards of half of the people who hire me to train their dogs have already taught their dog to sit and wait patiently for the bowl to be lowered to the ground, then wait for a release word to eat their meal.

The exercise we're going to do here is pretty similar, but we're also going to add in the eye contact exercise from earlier in the book to supercharge it. (I told you that would come in handy for lots of things later!)

This exercise is called slow treats and I believe the credit for inventing it goes to excellent clicker trainer Deb Jones.

Start off with your dog in front of you and a few treats in one hand. You will not need your clicker for this game.

Begin with your treat hand touching the same shoulder (for example, if you have treats in your left hand, hold them at the height of your left shoulder). Your arm should look a little bit like a cobra with its head reared back to strike.

When your dog is standing still, straighten your elbow and arc the treat-hand downward toward your dog's face—a cobra-strike delivering a treat to their lips instead of venom. (Take care to avoid intimidating your dog. If your dog is sensitive to fast movements around their face, move at a speed they are comfortable with, but the movement should be smooth and direct if possible.)

If your dog leans forward to meet your hand or bounces up to "help" you give them the treat, rapidly move your hand back to the starting position at your shoulder without giving them the treat. Whoops, missed an opportunity for a cookie!

The treat-cobra *only* strikes dogs who can wait calmly—just like the food bowl only lowers for a dog who can wait calmly.

You'll want to move pretty quickly at first so you're only asking for the dog to stay still for a second. Ideally, we don't want the dog to lean forward or "help" us in any way. Their only job is to be still in the time it takes the treat-cobra to strike.

If the dog can wait while you quickly lower the treat to them, put the treat directly into their mouth and reload the next treat.

For dogs who are a little sharky with fingers, it can be helpful to imagine that you want to deliver the treat about an inch inside of their mouth rather than right at their lips. We often subconsciously draw back at the last second to avoid having our fingers chomped, which actually makes the dog *more* likely to grab at fingers ("HEY, bring that back!").

It's normal to have a few errors where the dog tries to "help" you by leaning up to meet the treat, stretching their neck forward, or the occasional attempted chomp. While we're playing this game, those behaviors don't work, so don't pay for them. You don't need to fuss at your dog or make a big deal out of it—the removal of the treat is *plenty* of information for your dog to realize that they blew it. Good things come to those who wait.

And when you're taking the treat away, make sure you're taking it *all* the way back to the starting position. If your dog leans forward to "help" you feed them, the treat hand goes all the way back up to your shoulder to restart. If you just jerk it away a few inches, you're going to accidentally lure your dog into jumping up. That's frustrating for the dog, frustrating for you and it's going to take a lot longer to get where you need to go. Don't be tempted to hover your hand close to the dog or help them get it right at this stage. In reality, the most helpful thing you can do is make the contingencies crystal clear for your dog: If you wait, you get a cookie very quickly for doing nothing. If you reach for the cookie before it gets to you, you'll scare the treat-cobra all the way back up to the shoulder. We are trying to plant a seed in the dog's mind that self-control is a thing that can pay off even better than instant gratification.

Within a few repetitions, most dogs are willing to stand still for one to three seconds and wait for the treat to come to them if you move the treat briskly, which is great! "So, I literally just sit here and do nothing? And you'll just put treats directly into my mouth like I am a helpless baby bird? Gosh, my life of luxury is so hard."

Adding Eye Contact

Next, we're going to add in the eye contact component that we worked on earlier in the book. Remember how we waited for the dog to initiate eye contact, then captured that behavior with a treat so it would increase?

Start with your hand in treat-cobra position, but slightly off to the side of your shoulder so it's very clear whether your dog is looking at the treat-cobra hand or looking at your eyes. Wait until your dog makes eye contact with you like we did in the attention exercises, then rapidly begin to lower the treat toward your dog's face. Now it's your dog's responsibility to start the game by looking at you (and away from the treat), but you're still doing all of the work to deliver the treat. Your dog can initiate eye contact to turn on the slow treats game.

This requires a little bit more self-control, so even if your dog was a pro at the last stage, they may make errors here. This game requires them to look *away* from the thing that they want in order to get it. If the dog makes a grab for the treat, back up to your shoulder it goes and you'll wait for them to make eye contact again to restart the game. Your dog *does not* need to maintain eye contact the whole time as you lower the treat to them. The goal is for your dog to see something that they want, automatically look *away* from what they want to check in with you, and then receive a treat from you. You are the doorway to The Good Stuff.

Practice this several times until your dog is quickly able to look away from the treat in your hand at shoulder level and make eye contact with you to "ask" for it. Make sure you're putting the treat right into their lips so they don't have to do any steering at all. You want to keep practicing at this level until it stops looking "sticky" or like they can't quite drag their eyes away from the treat to look at you. Once they are easily looking away from the treat to find your eyes, you're ready to move on.

When your dog is doing the last step smoothly, gradually start to vary where you hold the treat. Instead of holding it at shoulder level, try holding your arm out to the side, above your head, rotated slightly behind you, and so on. Each time, your dog should glance at the treat they want, then make eye contact with you. As soon as they make eye contact, deliver the treat straight to their mouth.

Generally the higher and farther away from the dog the treat is, the easier it will be for your dog, so it is often helpful to start off higher and gradually work your way lower and closer to your dog as they are successful. If they make an error and try to go straight for the treat instead of asking with eye contact, the treat goes farther away. As usual, if they make more than two errors in a row, go back to an earlier step and rebuild from where they can be successful. We want your dog to be very confident that they know exactly what works (looking at you) and what doesn't (trying to reach the treat on their own in any way).

Once your dog can glance at the treat and immediately look up to make eye contact with you no matter where you hold the treat, it's time to move on!

Resisting Temptation

Now that your dog is beginning to understand the game, we're going to take it to the next level.

Outside of structured training sessions, unfortunately, the distraction that you're asking your dog to ignore is unlikely to be floating in the air at shoulder height out of range of dogs—but gosh, imagine how much easier that would make this lesson! In the real world, most of the things that tempt our dogs are right at nose level and most of the time, your dog is going to be closer to the contraband item than you are by the time you notice that they're tempted.

Dogs are opportunistic scavengers, which means that they are great at scavenging opportunistically. Foraging-for-junk behavior comes preinstalled, I'm afraid. That means that if we don't want that behavior, we need to manually uninstall it. That's what we're going to do in this section.

I like to think of temptations as having a sort of gravitational field—left to their own devices, an untrained dog will get sucked into the temptation like a black hole. The closer they get to the distraction, the stronger its gravitational pull is.

(If you've ever scrambled after a dog yelling "What's in your *mouth!*" then you probably already know what I mean about the black hole gravitational effect, and if you've never done that, then I don't believe you.)

When we started teaching your dog to look away from the treat to get the treat, we worked with the food at shoulder level so the gravitational field would be as weak as possible while your dog was figuring out what the game was. And when we started to vary the height and angle of the distraction, we started introducing the idea that the dog might have to go out of their way to *voluntarily* escape the gravitational field of the treat.

This next part is pretty cool. We're going to turn that gravitational field into a force field *protecting* the treat. Instead of pulling your dog in, we're going to turn the distraction into something that pushes them away.

Installing the Zen Force Field

Once your dog is a pro at holding eye contact even with a visible treat temptation in your hand, we're going to raise the difficulty level again by incorporating an exercise which trainers call "zen" (students of Sue Ailsby) or "it's yer choice" (students of Susan Garrett). The exercises are pretty much the same and the expressions are largely interchangeable.

This time, start with the treat in your fist rather than in your fingers. With your dog directly in front of you, hold your fist out off to your side at belly height, rotate your wrist so your palm is facing upward and flicker your hand open so the treat is briefly exposed flat on the palm of your hand. Your arm should look like a waiter holding a tray, but instead of a tray, it's one dog treat.

Be prepared to close your fist the instant your dog makes a dive for the treat, because this is a place where a lot of dogs make errors—and that's no surprise, when the treat gets exposed in the open right in front of them like that. In fact, work on the assumption that your dog *will* make an error the first few repetitions and be prepared to close your hand ASAP.

This time, if your dog makes a grab for it, instead of taking the treat back up to shoulder height, simply close your hand until they stop pestering the hand and make eye contact again. They should also move their head away from the treat hand in the process, even if it's just a tiny head bob away as they flick their gaze up to you.

If your dog is particularly zealous, your fingers may get nibbled here but it's typically gentle mouthing even with puppies who have poor mouth control. The more stationary you can hold your hand, the better—at this stage, you *don't* want to raise the treat back up to your shoulder and you don't want to move your hand away from the dog's mouth. It's very tempting to prompt the dog to leave your hand alone, but it's more effective to just show them that pestering the treat hand does not make the treat available.

The absolute second that your dog makes eye contact with you again ("Hey jerk, your hand is malfunctioning and it forgot to give me my treat, *do it again*"), flicker the hand open. If they instantly dive for it, close the hand again. If they back off and give you eye contact even for a fraction of a second, say "Yes!" and quickly put the treat into their mouth with the opposite hand.

Reload your hand with one treat.

Repeat this step until it looks smooth, being prepared to protect the treat any time you expose it. Don't worry about stretching the duration yet—we're just looking for a clear understanding that being able to see the treat *right there* is not an invitation to immediately eat it (which goes against everything that Mother Nature tells dogs about food). You absolutely do not want to accidentally teach the dog that making a lunge for the treat is a viable option!

Once your dog is able to maintain eye contact consistently when you open the hand for one second before you feed them, you can start to gradually increase the duration that your hand is open in front of their face. Again, this is a place where it can be really helpful to build up the duration in teeny tiny increments.

Gradually build up to about five seconds.

Once you have five seconds of duration, start varying the angle of your hand with each repetition, working gradually closer to your dog's face. If they pester the hand, it closes. If they can leave it alone and wait patiently, say "Yes" and give them the treat. Keep working at various angles until they can resist a treat right in front of their face *without* you having to close your hand to protect the treat.

At this stage, you should start to see a sort of force field effect happening. When you move the treat closer to their face, you can usually see them lean their head back a little bit or turn their chin off to the side to lower the level of temptation themselves. *That* is what we want to see! We are reinforcing subtle avoidance and they're starting to get it.

Once they are successfully ignoring a single treat right in front of their face until you deliver it to their mouth and you're not worried about your hand getting mobbed anymore, switch to having a small handful of treats in your hand at a time rather than one singular treat.

(No, an even *smaller* handful than that. About half of the amount that your hand can hold—about ten pieces at a time if you're using kibble. The fuller your hand is, the easier it is for a dog to jostle some treats loose by being rough or sudden, so a half-empty hand is much more secure than a bulging-full hand.)

When you open your hand this time with multiple treats in front of your dog, use your other hand to pick up one treat and deliver it to your dog's mouth.

If they make a dive for the treats or their impulse control is visibly wavering, close your zen hand and hold it still until they back off. Move the other hand back to a neutral position (i.e., don't hover with your non-treat hand in the air while waiting for them to back off the treat hand). As soon as they make eye contact again or visibly disengage from the treat hand, start to open the treat hand again.

If they're able to stay still while you deliver a treat from the treat hand, as soon as you've finished giving them the first treat, the treat-delivering hand should be moving back to the zen hand to get the next treat for your dog—these should be pretty rapidfire with minimal pauses between treats at this stage.

For example, if your left hand is holding the treats, your right hand should be quickly feeding one at a time from the left hand to your dog's mouth. If your dog tries to mob the left hand, the left hand closes to protect the treats and the right hand goes back to your side in a neutral position.

Once your dog is a pro at this, start gradually increasing the amount of time in between treats as the pile sits right in front of their face. For example, deliver a treat, pause one second with your hand open, deliver another treat, pause one second, another treat, and so on.

Attaching the Cue to Leave It

We're going to attach a cue to this behavior exactly the same way we attached it to potty in the last chapter. Before you begin to move your treat hand toward your dog's face, say the words "leave it" in a cheerfully neutral tone of voice, as if you were asking someone to please hold the door for you. Immediately after the cue, lower your hand as normal and reward your dog for ignoring the temptation of food right in front of their face. After giving them the treat, reload and start again, saying the cue "leave it" just before beginning to move. You want the word to be the first predictor that leaving temptations alone will pay off.

In the beginning, start with no duration at all. Once this looks solid, start building your duration back in, just like you did in the last section.

Then begin to generalize this to other surfaces. I like to start this skill when sitting down beside a hard raised surface such as a wooden coffee table. Don't choose the heirloom since there's a small chance that your dog will whack the table with their paws. It's important to use a rigid surface rather than a sofa cushion because sofa cushions tend to tip easily if jostled and drop treats everywhere—ask me how I've learned that.

This time, put a treat under your hand palm-down on the table surface, as if you've caught a fly under your hand. Quickly raise your hand just an inch or two to expose the treat, fully expecting to drop it down again if your dog dives toward the treat, which they are likely to do. Imagine that you just want to give them a peek at the treat-fly you've trapped under your hand, then cover it again before it can fly away. Be a good goalie and protect the treat, because this is a step where a lot of dogs start to make errors that they haven't made before. Constant vigilance!

It's normal for this step to be significantly harder than the exact same behavior with your hand.

Remember that possession is *at least* nine-tenths of the law for a dog. If the food is in your hand and you say that it's yours, dogs are like, "Meh, sure, it's probably yours." But if the same treat is just dropped on the *table* and you say that it's yours, your dog is going to do some quick physics calculations to decide whether they can nab it faster than you can defend it—which is exactly why we're teaching this skill in the first place. We want to teach them that no matter what their physics calculations tell them, we can always win, which is why we're stacking the deck in our favor.

As soon as your dog leaves your hand alone and either offers eye contact or visibly moves their head away from the treat, briefly uncover it again. If they dive for it, cover it.

If your dog can leave the treat alone for one second uncovered on the table, scoop the treat up and put it into their mouth. Reload, repeat.

Since your dog already has the general concept of "leave the covered treat alone to get a treat" from the previous lesson, they should pick up this skill faster the second time. Within a minute or two, they should deliberately back away from your hand and the uncovered treat. We want them to realize that the easiest way to get a treat is to pretend that they don't want it.

When your dog is solid with this, start to increase the amount of time you ask your dog to leave the treat alone and how far you move your hand away from the treat. Be conscious that you are gambling every time you raise the difficulty level. It pays to be a bit paranoid at this stage.

I am less fussy with full eye contact in the beginning here and more worried about duration of not-grabbing-the-treat, but if they offer me eye contact, I'll make the duration shorter. In other words, they can make me pay them faster by giving me full eye contact but it's not a hard requirement.

Gradually, I'll wait longer and longer in between treats and take my hand farther and farther away from the exposed treat as the dog becomes successful, but I'm always ready to protect the treat at a moment's notice.

Ideally, you want to see minimal frustration in this whole process. If you're getting vocalizing, pawing, hand-chewing or other fussing, you're probably asking for too much behavior too fast and it would benefit you to work on an easier step until your dog feels more confident in their skills. It pays to go slowly with dog training in general, but especially with a crucial skill like leave it.

Very Important! How to NOT Break This Behavior

At this stage, your dog knows how to leave distractions alone in very specific contexts where you are capable of preventing them from self-reinforcing. They've started to learn that "leave it" means that they will be paid to ignore something that they find tempting. This is huge.

But this *does not mean* that this skill is ready for use in the real world yet. In fact, trying to use this skill in the real world right now is almost guaranteed to break it.

Why? Because it's very easy to accidentally ask for more than your dog can actually do at this point, especially if you blurt "*leave it!*" reflexively as a Hail Mary when your dog is already inches away from the object of their desire. It *might* work if the challenge is within your dog's skill level. But if it doesn't, your dog just wrote themselves a big paycheck for doing the exact opposite of what you wanted them to do and that is a bigger risk with leave it than with most behaviors.

Think of it this way: Your dog has (a) evolutionary programming and (b) a lifetime of experiences, both of which teach your dog that the fastest way to get what they want is to help themself to it. We are essentially trying to teach them that the fastest way from Point A to Point B isn't a straight line anymore—it's through you.

We're teaching them that "leave it" means that they will be paid to ignore something that they find interesting. The other side of the coin is that we are simultaneously trying to build rock-solid faith that if you say "leave it," that means there is no way that your dog is capable of accessing the temptation anyway. To build that rock-solid faith, we need to manipulate the chances from the outside so that even a gambling dog realizes that this slot machine never, ever, ever pays. You want the message to be, "I am going to save you some effort and let you know that you cannot get that thing you want, even if it looks like you can. Total waste of energy, don't bother. You could test that theory and waste your own time or I'll pay you to ignore it. Your choice."

That means that any time you say "leave it" and they successfully get the thing that you asked them to leave, you are weakening the power of your "leave it" skill—and right now, it's a very young skill. And by now you know what we do with young skills, right? We build them slowly and carefully.

We're going to work up to greater levels of distraction and ask your dog to make more independent good choices later in the book when they genuinely *could* get the thing that we're asking them to leave. But for now, I'm asking you to only use your leave it cue when you can *guarantee* that your dog will not be able to get whatever you're asking them to leave, even if they make an error. They may try, but you'll be ready for them. In the meantime, continue to use management to keep your dog from engaging with distractions you can't control and practice resisting temptation with distractions that you can completely control.

Building A Stay: Duration, Distraction, Distance

Raising the Bar

At this point in your dog's training, you have several behaviors built up and are starting to attach cues to them. You have the beginning of a sit, a down, a settle on a mat, paws in a box, hand target, spin and eye contact—that's a great vocabulary for a beginner dog and plenty of variety to start moving forward with intermediate level skills.

You'll have noticed by now, of course, that these behaviors are all being taught to a fairly simple level. While it's convenient and polite, a two-second sit isn't going to do you an awful lot of good in the real world. And we're doing this training in the first place because you want your dog's real life skills to get better in ways that have a practical application, which means that it's time to level up the difficulty of the skills they already have.

In dog training circles, this is called "proofing," used in the same sense as proofing dough: making it sturdier and more complex. In old school training, proofing was done predominantly using corrections. The dog would be taught the baseline skill, such as the two-second sit above. Then the owner would ask for progressively longer stays and the training would consist of punishing the dog for leaving the sit before being released, often without making it sufficiently clear to the dog when they were allowed to move and when they would be corrected for doing so. Once the dog was deemed proficient, the trainer would start to layer in distractions and try to bait the dog into making a mistake (which would be punished). It was entirely the dog's responsibility to learn which words were distractions (meant to be ignored) and which were a release cue (meant to be obeyed). That trial-and-error process involved quite a lot of error—and with it, quite a lot of corrections. In addition to being unfair to the dog, this is just plain inefficient. You may get to a functional stay faster in the first place, but you'll be forever duct taping it back together with "reminders" when it comes unglued, and stressing your dog out in the process.

We now know how to build up a dog's skills gradually and incrementally so that the dog's ability level matches what we ask of them.

To put it in human terms, the old school method was like giving a kid a dictionary and calling that teaching them how to read. Yes, technically they have the resources, but what a slog! There are kinder ways to raise the bar.

Boiling Frogs in Dog Training

You may have noticed the theme by now that when we're changing things, we change them gradually.

In dog training, we call this incremental change **splitting** out criteria (as opposed to **lumping**, which is asking for large chunks of behavior at a time—very tempting for humans but very confusing for dogs). Good dog trainers are good splitters. The more finely you can break down the skill, teach the individual component as a bite-sized piece and then stitch the components back together, the more efficient your dog training will be.

Incidentally, this also works on people. For example, the book you are reading now was written in 400-word chunks instead of the 2,000-word chapters I prefer because bite-sized behavior is easier to perform even when it adds up to the same overall end point. Writing a whole book is a *huge* behavior, but writing 400 words at a time is perfectly reasonable. Reaching your training goals can be similar.

We often use the analogy that raising the difficulty in dog training is like boiling frogs. Personally, I have never boiled a frog, so I'm working on theory here, but the fable goes that when boiling a frog, the goal is to put live frogs into a pot of water and raise the temperature so gradually that the frogs don't notice the change in temperature as it rises. If you drop a live frog into a pot of already-boiling water, they'll just hop out, but if you put them into cool water and gradually heat it, they will adjust to the changes incrementally and won't realize the water is warming up until it's too late.

Well, that was morbid. Sorry, frog-lovers. It's just a fable.

We can think of dog training in similar ways. We want to start off with the skill as easy as it can possibly be, then gradually bump up the difficulty level a hair at a time so the dog's experience level grows with the challenge—without the dog realizing that we are gradually making it harder and harder.

When leveling up a skill, make sure to only work on one component of the behavior at a time for maximum growth. Just like a targeted strength training at the gym gives you a better workout in those body parts than general movement, being more specific and thoughtful about the way that you increase the challenge in your training will allow you to build your dog's skills quickly. It's easier for your dog to build "muscle" if you're only targeting one layer of difficulty at a time, even though that may feel slower in the short term.

For most behaviors, we break these skills into three major sections: duration, distraction and distance. **Duration** is how long the dog needs to do the behavior to be rewarded, **distraction** is how difficult the external situation is, and **distance** is how far apart the components are.

For each skill, we are going to build each component individually. For example, we might do one session with sit + duration (a sit-stay), then a session with hand target + distance (come when called) and then a session with a settle + distraction (calm in difficult environments). As your dog masters each component individually, we'll stitch them together for a rock-solid behavior that will hold up to even the most difficult real-world distractions.

Building Duration

The first type of proofing we're going to work on is building duration. The general principles here work with any sort of skill, but in this case, we're going to talk about a sit-stay as an example behavior. You can apply the same steps to a down-stay, a "sticky" nose target (press-and-hold), multiple turns in your spin, extended eye contact and so on.

When I'm teaching a stay, I start off without using a stay cue at all. As with all of the training in this book, I want to get the skill really solid before I label the behavior. I always want the cue to be attached to the finished product behavior, not the work in progress. Stay is a behavior that I see a lot of people break by pushing it too far too early—the more patient you can be with this one, the better off you'll be in the long run.

Ask your dog to sit, then immediately click and give them a treat as usual, delivering the treat right to their mouth. Before they have a chance to stand up, while they're still chewing the first treat, click and treat a second time. Repeat this three or four more times, then say "Release" and toss a treat off to the side.

(As a side note, I am okay with using the cue "release" very early in the process because I am willing to bet my $20 that if you throw a treat off to the side, your dog is going to follow it. The exception proves the rule. Don't use your other cues this early.)

Repeat this sequence a couple of times, giving five to ten click/treats for the same sit for as long as your dog is sitting, and then saying "Release" and tossing a treat away to reset your dog to begin again.

Once this feels fluid and your dog is happily expecting multiple treats for the same sit, you can start to gradually stretch the increment between treats. Start off by adding a one-second pause between some of the treats but keeping some of the others immediate, then release and reset. In the next set, add in some two-second pauses and some one-second pauses and keep some of the click/treats immediate.

That variability is important. You don't want to increase the difficulty level of all of them across the board, for example one second between all of the treats, then two seconds between all of the treats, then three seconds between all of the treats, and so on. Remember to raise the temperature gradually! If you make it continuously harder and harder and your dog can predict that it's only going to get more difficult, some dogs will get frustrated with you and quit earlier in the process. But if some of the treats are immediate and then there is a variable amount of time to wait for the next treat, the dog is always on the edge of their seat because it could be just *one* more second before the click and treat.

So keep it variable and keep it easy in the beginning. You can get a lot of mileage on your stays working with very short durations. It's better to have a rock-solid ten-second stay than a wobbly thirty-second stay.

As you level up this skill, keep the amount of time variable, but start to increase the distance between all of the treats over time. For example, a more experienced dog might get clicks/treats at eight seconds, two seconds, thirteen seconds, nine seconds, four seconds, six seconds, twelve seconds. That's an average of eight seconds but with a range from two to thirteen seconds so the dog never knows when the next click is coming.

If your dog stands up before you've reached the goal number, they don't get a release treat. Just reset them into the sit and begin the count again. If you get multiple errors in a row, lower the difficulty level to the point where your dog can easily succeed, then build forward again, or end the session and come back later. Multiple errors are usually either a sign that you are raising the criteria too fast for your dog's ability level or that your dog is fatigued. At this stage, the whole session should be no more than a few minutes long.

The beginning stages of this are where most of your errors will be and it pays to be thorough from day one. It may seem trivial to work on a three-second stay in your living room with high value treats when you eventually want a ten minute stay in the middle of a public park with no treats, but these foundations are worth investing in.

Building Distraction

Distraction-proofing is my favorite type of proofing and you can't change my mind.

We've been doing most of your preliminary training in a familiar, low-distraction environment because that's what a beginner dog's skill level can handle the most easily—it's easiest to level up your dog's skills when they're not also using half of their brain to filter out all of the unrelated stimuli going on around them. In the beginning, you want all of the brain-resources allocated to learning the skill itself.

But the real world has distractions and if you want your dog to be able to listen in complex environments with a lot of moving parts, then you need to build that skill gradually so they will be able to perform under pressure.

Ready? This one is a fun one.

When I'm proofing for distractions with a relatively new cue, I like to play a game called "What would a fidgety three-year-old do right now?" And since I am secretly a three-year-old at heart, this is an endless source of entertainment for me. It's sort of like Simon Says, but on single-player mode.

For the purposes of this exercise, we're using a sit again, but it could be nearly any behavior that your dog already knows.

The setup goes like this. Ask your dog to sit, click/treat. While they're still sitting, turn your head to the right and click as your head turns—not after, but during. Immediately turn back to your dog and give them a treat. Lift one foot slightly, click/treat. Raise an arm in the air, click/treat. Say the word "aardvark," click/treat. Touch your nose, click/treat. In the beginning, you are clicking *while* doing the distracting behavior, not afterward, so the dog *almost* doesn't have enough time to make an error because you're clicking before they've even had a chance to process that you've done something strange.

After a few repetitions, say, "Release" and toss a treat to give your dog a chance to take a breath. This is mentally taxing for dogs, so short sessions with frequent breaks are helpful. Reset your dog in a sit again and continue.

Some dogs tend to be more high-energy and distractible—the littlest thing makes them go bouncing off across the room. (I live with a houseful of high-energy herdy dogs, so these types are my favorite!) In those cases, I make my distraction movements very brief and click as early in the distraction as I possibly can so the amount of time they need to be correct is extremely short. Good distractions for these types of dogs include small head motions, picking up one foot at a time, a quarter turn of the torso, touching your nose, putting your hand on the top of your head, crossing your arms across your chest like a mummy, scratching your ear, putting your hands in your pockets, bending at the waist, touching your knees, and so on. These are small movements that build toward the concept that a person moving does not mean that the dog should also be moving, and that staying in their sit is still the most reinforcing thing to do at this point. Make sure you are always delivering the treat directly to your dog's mouth for these exercises so they don't have to think any movement thoughts at all, even about getting their cookie.

Other dogs tend to be more low-energy and forgiving, and you can build up distractions more quickly with these dogs. In addition to the list above, these are the dogs who will let you jog in place, touch your toes, spin in a circle, do a jumping jack, wave your arms in the air, drum on your belly, sit in a chair, knock on the wall/door and a huge variety of more active distractions. While the more distractible dog above will get there with time, some dogs will let you get away with these more difficult distractions right off the bat because they're simply slower to get up once "stuck" in a stay. Test more active distractions like this carefully at first by beginning with the safe list in the previous paragraph and only moving on to these once your dog is responding well.

And have fun! You get to goof off and train your dog at the same time. Sometimes we all need permission to take the world less seriously.

You can get creative with your distractions once your dog has a solid foundation in these skills. I like to bounce tennis balls past my dogs in a stay, open and close doors, open and close the fridge, pick up and put down their food bowl, dance or do yoga, and so on.

But for now, have fun with the beginner level distractions and see what your dog can ignore! Remember, we're working on duration and distance separately, so these should be quick, one-second distractions right beside the dog for this section. We'll combine all of them to level them up together later in the chapter.

If your dog stands up or leaves their stay, they miss out on a chance for a cookie and you now have information that the challenge level was too high for them. Is there a way you can break that distraction level in half? For example, if you tried to touch your toes and your dog stood up out of their sit, can they hold a sit if you bend your shoulders? What about if you bend your shoulders and wiggle your arms? What if you bend your shoulders and touch your knees? Touch your shins? Touch your ankles? *Now* can they hold a stay when you touch your toes?

Building Distance

Distance is typically the criterion that most people start training first with their stays and it's the *last* component that I work on when I am teaching a stay.

Why?

Because distance fundamentally requires some level of duration and distraction. It takes time to walk toward/away from your dog and movement is inherently distracting for most dogs. If I haven't already built that foundation, I'm asking my dog to handle all three components at once without a lot of context for how to get it right. In other words, I am setting my dog up to fail. Yikes!

So now I work on distance after my dog already has some experience with distractions and duration separately. It doesn't need to be much experience, but some. I've usually worked up to at least ten seconds of duration and distractions equivalent to touching my toes or turning around in a circle without the dog looking tempted to stand up—once I have that much, that's enough to start building for distance.

The formula for building distance is clicking at the apex of the distance, then returning to give the dog the treat—similar to how we clicked *during* the distraction for the distraction portion.

To begin, lift one foot briefly, immediately click, put the foot down and feed the treat, just like you would do if you were using lifting-a-foot as your distraction behavior in the previous section. Then take a partial step back with one foot but keep your weight balanced on the planted foot—imagine that you are testing the ground behind you to see if it is solid enough to hold your weight but not really planning to step on it. Click as you plant the moving foot, then immediately put it back in starting position and pay the dog. It should look a little bit like a fidgety dance move.

Then take your first full step backward, rocking back on your heel, clicking, stepping forward and delivering the treat. Splitting up the first step may seem like splitting hairs, but it reduces a lot of preventable errors which means more clarity for your dog and faster progress for you.

In the beginning, stay facing your dog and move one step backward, click, one step forward, pay. Step back, click, forward, pay. Repeat this a few times, varying the angle slightly so you're a bit on the diagonal on some reps and straight ahead on others. Next, try mixing in sideways steps instead of just backward. Sidestep to the left, click, return to center, pay. Sashay to the right, click, return to center, pay. Then start mixing in some two-step repetitions, again clicking at the furthest point and returning to feed your dog.

Once you've worked up to about five steps like that and your dog does not look like they are sitting on the edge of their seat dying to stand up every time you move, start building in the turn component. You want them to look pretty solidly planted in place before you add this component in. Start off right in front of your dog and pivot 90 degrees, click, pay. Repeat in the opposite direction. If this looks good, practice a 180 degree pivot in both directions, click, pay. On the next rep, pivot 180 degrees and take one step away from your dog, click, immediately return, pay. Turning your back on your dog significantly raises the difficulty for most dogs.

It's tempting to add a bunch of distance very quickly, but it's worth it to babysit this skill for a little bit. It's better to have a solid foundation built slowly than a shaky foundation built quickly. And remember that each component should be built separately, so avoid building in distractions or duration this early in the process—the more cleanly you can isolate the skill that you're trying to build, the faster it will level up.

Oops! Troubleshooting Errors

Somewhere in this process, even the best dog with the best trainer is going to make an error. That's fine! That's just another opportunity to learn.

The general response to errors when raising the difficulty level is to just reset the dog and try again. If you get two errors in a row, or if you're under a roughly 80% success rate, you're asking for more than your dog can give you right now. Lower the difficulty level to the point where you are absolutely confident that they can be successful and build forward from there.

For some people, this can feel disheartening, as if they're losing progress. In reality, what you're doing is adding layers of understanding to solidify your dog's skills. The fact that he could do it yesterday does not mean that he can do it today, especially in the very early stages when your dog is still figuring out what you want and how to get it right. Be generous, be forgiving and be willing to take the scenic route in the beginning. Right now, you're not just teaching a four-second sit-stay—you're teaching the entire *concept* of a stay.

It's also worth double-checking how long you've been training. It's easy to lose track of time when working on stays and an increasing number of errors can be a sign of mental fatigue. Setting a timer on your phone for a five- to ten-minute training session can be helpful for keeping yourself honest about how long your dog has been working. If you notice that you're getting a lot more errors at the end of a session, that's information that your dog may benefit from shorter training sessions more frequently instead of long training sessions.

Combining Criteria

Once your dog has made progress on each of the individual proofing exercises, you can start to weave them together to create more realistic training challenges.

When you do this, make sure you lower the difficulty level of each component part significantly below your dog's current skill level. In other words, remember that you're effectively doubling the difficulty by working on multiple components, so make sure you halve the difficulty in the individual criteria when you combine them. If your dog has a ten-second stay for duration and also a ten-step stay for distance and you want to combine those together, you'd start off with a five-second stay at five feet, for example—or possibly even closer or shorter depending on your dog's needs. Then systematically build up from there.

Work on each pair individually before combining the full system together and beginning to incorporate real-life distractions.

I like to think of my distractions as either "wild" or "tame." "Tame" distractions are the ones that I can control, such as bouncing a ball, and "wild" distractions are the ones that I can't control, such as small children making small-child noises in the next room.

When I'm intentionally trying to stretch my dog's skills, I'm going to prioritize working with "tame" distractions as much as I possibly can because that's how I can get the maximum bang for my distraction buck without pushing my dog too far and causing them to make an error. The ability to fine-tune my own distractions means I can make progress faster, even if it feels more artificial in the beginning. When we face "wild" distractions, I want to be confident that my dog is over-prepared to deal with the challenge level because I am less able to manipulate wild distractions to match my dog's skill level.

And remember that it's almost always easier for dogs to perform when they're warmed up, so the place where you ended yesterday's session is probably significantly more advanced than where you should begin today's. Give them a few easy reps to get their brain booted up, then start to stretch their skills from there.

Generalizing and Proofing

Generalists and Specialists

Humans are great at generalizing. We're excellent at recognizing categories of things and sorting novel experiences into those categories. If you've ever met a toddler who thinks everything furry and brown with four legs is "doggie," you've seen generalization in action.

Dogs are the opposite. Dogs are specialists. They are excellent at finding the differences between things and developing context-specific responses to each. This is both a blessing and a curse.

As it relates to dog training, it's more often a curse than a blessing, because it means that your cues may not be what you think they are. It's possible to accidentally build in additional parts of the cue that you hadn't intended to be part of the picture. For example, you may think that your cue is the word "down," but if your dog thinks that the cue is the word "down" plus a downward tilt of your chin plus a treat in your hand plus pointing at the floor, they're going to look at you like you're crazy when you ask for that same down in the middle of the park with only the verbal cue.

If you've ever groaned, "But he *knows* it at home!" then you've seen a specialist in action.

In practical terms, what that means is that we have to do a few extra steps to make sure that the skills we've taught will translate to real-world situations. We want to strengthen the cues that we *want* to be attached to the behavior and simultaneously undermine or erase the cues that might get attached due to environmental factors.

In other words, we're making it obvious to the dog how to filter out which part of the cue is relevant and what's just background noise.

Generalizing to New Environments

Generalizing to new environments is the easiest generalization project to start and the most difficult to finish because of the wide variety of environmental factors that can change dramatically depending on where you train.

The beginning part is easy, though. Ready?

Take the skills that we worked on in the previous sections and re-teach them in a new room in your house. If you taught them in the living room, start from scratch and re-teach them in the kitchen.

Then do the same thing in the bathroom.

And a bedroom.

And the front porch.

And the backyard.

Usually by about the fifth new location, you'll see a little lightbulb go on over the dog's head. "Hold on a second! I might be crazy, but it seems like this is *exactly the same behavior* that I already know in four other places. So are you telling me that the sound 'down' means I should lie down no matter where I am and what type of surface I'm standing on and which direction the door is and how my person is oriented to me?"

Yep, that's exactly what I'm telling you, pup!

But in the beginning, you're going to reteach from scratch in each new environment as if they'd never heard this cue before in their life and build forward from there.

Reteaching the skill from scratch is going to shore up any weak areas in your foundation and make the resulting behavior much stronger than if you just tried to move the finished skill into new locations. You *can* do that, but it's cutting corners and it'll show up in the behavior eventually. How much that matters to you is your decision. But for my own dogs, I aim to teach each new skill from the ground up in five completely different places—and if I can make those places very different, I do. Some example locations to get you started: your front yard, your driveway, a parking lot, the vet's office, a pet store, a pet-friendly home improvement store, the beach, a baseball game, a friend's house, a random parking lot and so on.

For maximum efficiency, I start off using simpler environments and work up to more complex environments once the dog already has the skill in an easier location.

Proofing Handler Positions

The next component is to generalize for handler positions, which can also be a lot of fun. I treat this one kind of like a scavenger hunt where I try to pick as many different positions of my body as possible to practice the same cue. For example, if I am proofing a sit, I'll cue it while standing up. If the dog does, click and treat. I'll sit on a chair and cue again, click/treat if correct. Then sit on the ground and cue again. Then I'll lie on the sofa and cue again. Then I'll turn 90 degrees away from my dog so they're facing my hip instead of facing me directly and cue again. (Did they come sit in front of you instead? Reset and try again; the goal is for them to sit where they are. You may need to face a wall or obstacle to prevent them from moving to the front of you the first few times you practice this). Then facing completely away. Then

with my hands on my head. Then with my arms in the air. Then with my hands on my hips. While jogging in place. With one foot lifted like a flamingo. While touching my toes.
 Does this sound ridiculous? Yep.
 Does this look ridiculous? Yep.
 Is it effective in training a dog? Also yep.
 Plus it is secretly kind of fun, but don't tell anyone.

Cue Discrimination

Most of what we've done so far has been drilling the same skill back to back. At this point, we're going to start mixing it up so your dog has to *think* about which behavior you're asking for. This is a great exercise for "taking the temperature" of your cues to see what's sticking and what needs more work.

In the beginning, it will be beneficial to help more than you think you'll need to.

Start off with the two cues that your dog knows best. For most dogs, this is going to be a hand target and a sit, but your mileage may vary depending on what you've put the most work into. Bounce back and forth between these two skills unpredictably, sometimes repeating either cue a few times in a row, sometimes alternating one-two-one-two. If your dog gets it right, click and treat. If your dog makes an error, pause for three seconds, then give the cue again with a bit more help, such as adding the lure back in to get them back on the right track.

If you're getting multiple errors in a row, go back to an earlier difficulty level and work forward again.

Once your dog is a pro at these two skills, add a third skill into rotation, for example your down. Then a fourth, such as go to mat. And a fifth, such as leave it.

And be particularly conscious of your patterns. For example, the vast majority of my students automatically do sit first, then down. Don't enable a cheater-dog! Make sure you mix it up so they have to *listen* to the cue instead of just guessing.

Not only is this going to improve your dog's mental flexibility and ability to switch between tasks, it's also going to slightly level up each of the individual skills you work on because being able to discriminate between a sit and a down makes both of those individual skills more distinct and the line between them less blurry for your dog.

Differential Reinforcement: Jumping Prevention

What Is Differential Reinforcement and Why Should You Care?

Differential reinforcement is like a sliding scale of reinforcement—if X is proportionally more reinforcing than Y, the behavior is going to shift toward X even if Y is still better than nothing.

For example, if you'd get paid $100 for one behavior and $5 for another behavior and you only get to choose one or the other, you're probably going to do the $100 behavior and the $5 behavior is going to decrease proportionally even though it technically pays. The person paying doesn't need to punish the $5 behavior itself—they just need to make the other option the obvious better choice.

Differential reinforcement is really effective for working around behaviors which the environment is going to pay to some degree, and the king of those behaviors is jumping.

I would say that probably a fifth of my training business comes from dogs who jump on guests at the door. Jumping is a perfectly natural greeting behavior for dogs, who instinctively want to move closer to faces. And it doesn't help that the majority of the things that we humans instinctively do to stop a dog from jumping (talking to them, looking at them, touching them, moving into their space, getting loud and excited) gives them exactly the attention they were asking for. In many cases, our attempts to decrease the jumping are actually the reinforcement that maintains it and we'd be better off doing nothing!

But even the most dog-loving person doesn't want paw-print-shaped bruises, and frankly, many of the dogs who are jumping all over the guests are more frantic than happy, so they're often not enjoying the greeting as much as they could either—especially if the end result is getting fussed at or put away every time guests come over.

So instead, let's harness the power of differential reinforcement to teach your dog that a different behavior pays better than jumping.

Teaching Four on the Floor

You'll need your dog, a door, a leash, a full treat bag and a volunteer guest with fifteen minutes to spare. (If you don't have a family member who can be the "visitor," then offer to pay a friend in pizza—they will say yes.)

Our first priority is to physically prevent the dog from self-reinforcing for jumping, which means finding a management step to use as training wheels. Every time your dog successfully puts paws on a person, imagine that they are writing a tiny paycheck to themselves for jumping. If we want to convince them that jumping does not pay off, it's easier if we prevent them from writing that check. A leash or a baby gate is usually your best bet. Even if your dog gets it wrong and *tries* to jump, they should not be able to successfully make contact with the guest. If jumping is a problem for your dog, they probably have a solid learning history that jumping is reinforcing already and we don't want to put any more weight on that end of the see-saw than we have to. For the rest of these instructions, I'll assume you are using a leash.

Ask the guest to walk in the door without knocking or ringing the doorbell, both of which are likely to be conditioned triggers for even more excited behavior from your dog. Standing ten feet away from the door and out of leash's reach of your guest, begin clicking and treating your dog for any second when all four of their feet are on the floor. I find it most effective to deliver the reinforcement to the floor by dropping it right between the dog's front paws, which has the added bonus of keeping them looking down at the floor instead of gazing adoringly into your guest's eyes and thinking about full-body tackling them with love.

Your clicker should sound like a machine gun: click-click-click-click. In the beginning, we're not asking for any duration at all, so any second where all four feet are stationary is clickable and payable.

The guest should stand in the doorway and look at your ceiling without talking, looking at the dog or engaging with either of you. "My, what a nice ceiling fan you have. I am an incredibly boring person and I have never seen such a lovely ceiling fan," should be their body language. It may help for them to cross their arms across their chest to signal even more firmly with their body language that they are not here to interact with the dog.

After a few seconds, have the guest go back outside and count to thirty. This will give your dog a second to collect their brain and stop pumping adrenaline if they're used to greetings at the door being the exciting highlight of their day.

Have the guest come back inside. Same thing: any second of stillness is clickable.

If you're not getting stillness at all, you're either way too close to the door for your dog's skill level or your guest is probably looking at or talking to the dog. Give your dog more distance from the guest and remind your guest to be as boring as they can.

As your dog stays successful, gradually reduce the distance between you and the guest, moving forward in tiny increments and pausing long enough for your dog to collect their brain each time before you move closer again. You will probably see a sort of "extra strong gravity" effect taking over where your dog's eyes are glued to the ground and they seem to be standing more rigidly than normal, like a rocking-horse position. This is common when they're waiting for a treat to appear on the floor and have decided to skip the middleman (looking at you) to go straight to the source (looking at the ground). In this case, that's desirable, because it's very hard to jump on a person and stare at the ground at the same time, although I'm sure there are some dogs who could manage.

Finally, once your guest can stand right next to your dog while your dog ignores them for treats from the floor, have your guest begin to *gently, slowly* and *in the most boring way possible* pet your dog along the sides of their ribs—not the top of the head and not along the back, because those are more likely to invite more jumping. Along the sides of the shoulders and ribs are usually the best bet for most dogs.

If your dog jumps, you and the guest should step away from each other in opposite directions. "Sorry, pup! We switched the rules and what used to be the forward button is now the reverse!" Instead of getting social reinforcement, your dog loses access to the person by jumping. Sometimes it is helpful to think of the jumping "pushing them right out the door." Have the guest go outside for at least another thirty seconds before coming back in, then restart at an easier level where your dog can be successful.

For as long as your dog is able to stand politely and not boil over with excitement, the guest can pet the dog. As soon as the dog tries to jump or becomes frantic, the guest leaves, the dog goes back to the far side of the room and you start over again.

The initial goal is for the guest to be able to walk in very calmly and briefly pet your dog for two or three seconds while you initially stuff treats into your dog's face for keeping their feet planted on the ground.

Remember that a dog with a jumping problem has been paid *well* and *frequently* for jumping in the past. We need to both unplug access to that reinforcer by making jumping difficult *and* outweigh it with a staggering amount of reinforcement on the behavior that we do want to see, which is standing or sitting calmly in the presence of guests. I promise you will not need to make it rain chicken every time you have guests over forever, but in the beginning, there's really no such thing as too much.

You want the message to your dog to be twofold: First, jumping no longer works, so don't bother. In fact, the only thing jumping does now is make the person leave the room, which is the opposite of what the dog wants. And second, you would have to be a blooming idiot to do anything other than stand here and open your mouth for the buffet.

As your dog gets more experienced with this, you can taper down the food rewards until the petting from the guest is the primary reward and you're just using food intermittently for particularly good choices, but in the beginning, it pays to be generous.

Something you may accidentally learn in this exercise is that dogs are often easier to train than humans. Most people will find the "helper" behaviors very hard to perform—after all, they love dogs enough that they offered to help you train yours. If your chosen helper is proving to be less than helpful for this exercise, end the session when it's clear that they aren't able to do what you ask (because trying to teach this using an excitable human is very likely to put weight on the wrong side of the behavioral see-saw), thank them mightily for their help, and hand over the pizza anyway—they did try. If it helps, you can also remind yourself that you have probably differentially reinforced your friend for somewhat calmer behavior than their normal hyper greeting with dogs, because the opportunity to help a friend, see a dog and eat pizza is almost certainly more valuable than just petting dogs briefly. Then ask a different person to help next time. Someone who is dog-neutral may actually be a better helper for this exercise than a dog-lover.

Once your dog is doing great with this on leash and can go through a whole greeting without ever attempting to jump, try the same thing without the leash—but do make sure that your dog is solidly successful on leash first to avoid the preventable errors. Raise your rate of reinforcement to blindingly fast again and have your guest step outside the door any time the dog does jump. Reteach until the skill is solid both on and off leash. Once your dog understands the contingency, you can taper down the food reinforcement and rely more heavily on social reinforcers from the guests. After all, we know social attention from guests is a potent reinforcer for your dog because it was successfully paying for the jumping behavior in the first place.

Congratulations! You've decreased the behavior of jumping by increasing the behavior of standing with four feet planted on the ground.

# 4

Leash Manners

Loose Leash Walking

Your Graduation Project

In the beginning of the book, you learned the primary skills you'll need to teach almost any behavior. You know how to get the initial behavior with luring, capturing, targeting or shaping. If you use a lure, you know how to fade it. You can attach a cue, proof for distractions, generalize to new environments and decrease unwanted behaviors with differential reinforcement of the alternative.

Phew! You've learned a lot! Pat yourself on the back for sticking with the process this long. The information you've learned this far can be applied to almost any behavior you want to teach your dog to do and your proverbial training toolbox is well stocked.

Now we're going to take those skills for a test drive so you can see how they all apply to building the most commonly requested behavior in my training classes: walking politely on a loose leash without pulling.

By the end of this chapter, you'll have a dog so well-trained that a walk in the park really *feels* like a walk in the park.

Ready? Let's get started.

Why Most Dogs Pull

If I had a nickel for every time someone said that they "just" wanted to work on pulling, I could afford to retire.

This is far and away the most common behavior I'm asked to fix, and for good reason: it's time-consuming to teach and easy to break if you're not being careful.

The environment is full of interesting things that dogs want to see. That's why we take them on walks in the first place: because seeing the world is valuable to most dogs. And if pulling on the leash successfully gets them closer to those things, then access to those things is slowly-but-continuously reinforcing your dog for pulling on a leash. And since the average human walks significantly slower than the average dog (half the number of legs, y'know), we're already at a disadvantage from day one.

You would think that pressure on the collar would be enough to stop a dog from pulling and in most cases you would be wrong. There are a few dogs who are naturally light on the leash and find collar pressure more unpleasant than the world is desirable, but that list is surprisingly short. Left to their own devices and with enough opportunities to practice, most dogs are passively shaped to pull to get where they want to go. The default setting is slowly working against you if you're not actively trying to prevent it.

And to make matters worse, most of the things that we automatically do to reduce pulling actually make it worse. Pulling backward against a dog's neck often makes them dig in harder. Allowing them to haul us around for extended periods of time ("to wear them out, because a tired dog is a good dog") just puts more mileage on the pulling behavior that we're trying to prevent.

I don't want to manage my dog with gear or punish the pulling out of them—I want them to happily choose to walk with me on a loose leash without threat or coercion. After all, the reason I'm walking them in the first place is because I love them and want the best for them.

By Your Powers Combined

The cool thing about loose leash walking is that it's not just one behavior. You can't define it as "not-pulling." We call that a **dead-dog behavior**, which means that it isn't actually a behavior at all—it's the absence of behavior. An easy test to check whether you need to reframe your training goal is to ask yourself if a scarecrow, stuffed animal or dead dog can do the behavior you're trying to train (such as not-pull, not-jump, not-bark). Remember, it's much faster to teach a dog exactly what they *should* do instead of eliminating every possible behavior they *shouldn't* do.

So, what does not-pulling look like? Well, it looks like voluntarily choosing to walk within 4–6 feet of me while connected by a leash in a variety of environments, to respond to any incidental collar pressure by moving toward me instead of leaning against the pressure away from me, to move away from distractions when asked and to move through space at roughly the same speed I'm walking, including stopping when I stop and going when I go.

When you put it that way, it sounds pretty complicated, doesn't it?

But that description is also very specific, which means that we can tease apart that definition and work on each chunk of the behavior individually. Our goal isn't just for you to have a dog who "doesn't pull"—it's for you to have a dog who voluntarily and happily chooses to walk politely by your side at any speed in any environment without management, "reminders" or specific gear to keep them on track, because they've learned that that's just the place to be when walking.

Captured Heel Position

Kindergarten: Indoors, Off Leash

By now, you're familiar with the kindergarten analogy and the concept that we want to start training in an easy environment before moving toward more difficult situations.

You might be surprised to learn that for loose leash walking, kindergarten is both indoors and off leash.

A lot of dogs with an extensive pulling history are already doing undesirable behaviors before you've even gotten out the door, and some have learned that the leash itself is a cue to launch forward as fast as possible. If you've ever been physically hauled through your own doorway, you know what I'm talking about.

So instead, we're going to start where you are almost guaranteed to be successful and work forward from there.

We're going to teach your dog the individual components of loose leash walking as stand-alone skills, then stitch the skills together and add a leash as a seatbelt, not a steering wheel. This will allow us to teach the new habits quickly without having to wade through your dog's current behavioral repertoire while we're trying to build the new one. There's no sense in putting more mileage on pulling while working to build an alternative.

Loose Leash Walking Equipment

The leash and collar aisle of your local pet store is overflowing with quick-fix equipment options which promise instant loose leash walking, and I can guarantee you that I've seen a dog pull through all of it. You name it, I've seen a dog pulling while wearing it.

So we're skipping that part.

For the purposes of this book, you'll need a regular flat collar or martingale collar (for dogs with heads skinnier than their necks, to prevent the collar from slipping over their heads), a regular six-foot leash with a snap (in other words, not a slip lead, long line or retractable leash), a treat pouch, a selection of very high value treats and your clicker.

Optionally, if your dog already has an entrenched pulling habit, you may also want a front-attach harness (ideally one which doesn't have a strap straight across the front of the chest). While this won't take the place of training, a front-attach harness can help to redirect your dog back toward you when they reach the end of the leash—especially for overzealous large-breed dogs who can otherwise be difficult to walk safely. For harnesses, I like the Ruffwear Front Range, the PetSafe 3-in-1, the Freedom harness or the Blue-9 Balance harness, all of which you'll likely need to order online as they can be hard to find in stores. I like these specific brands because they are very adjustable and low-impact even if your dog hits the end of the leash in a hurry.

What Goes in Which Hand

Just like with the clicker exercises at the beginning of the book, we're going to start off without your dog, because your physical mechanics here can make a huge difference in how easy this skill is for you in the long term.

We're going to teach your dog to walk on your left side. Left is a convention that comes from formal obedience trainers for competitions. There's nothing inherently *better* about walking your dog on the left rather than the right, but all of the instructions are going to assume that's what you're doing, so if you don't want to have to flip everything, pick left and be consistent.

Get your leash, clicker, treat pouch and bowl again, because we're going to practice your leash mechanics before adding the dog in.

Remember how we practiced delivering treats to the substitute-dog bowls earlier in the book? We're going to revisit that now, plus a leash. Place a bowl at roughly dog-face-height beside your left knee.

Then put your filled treat pouch on your left hip, straight above the substitute-dog bowl.

Put your right wrist through the loop of the leash so that the leash passes across your palm and between your thumb and forefinger. This is your emergency brake. Like the emergency brake on your car, it's for emergencies—you should not be using it regularly while "driving" your dog, but it's good to have it if you need it.

Place your clicker on top of the leash in your right hand. I find a wrist coil very helpful for holding my clicker so I can drop and pick up my clicker without actually *dropping* my clicker, but that's optional. The top of your leash should be sandwiched between your palm on the bottom and the clicker on top. You can let the clip of the leash dangle down to your imaginary dog.

Now use your left hand to very lightly hold the leash about halfway down the leash's length with your palm up as if accepting a gift. This is your steering wheel and your normal brake as well as your treat hand. This hand will slide up and down the length of the leash as needed to keep the tension on the line correct, and it will also dispense treats when the right hand clicks.

Begin with the leash draped across the left palm at about the halfway point so that you have a U of leash between your two hands. Click with the right hand, drop the leash with the left, use the left hand to deposit a treat into the bowl, then re-drape the leash across your left hand. Your right hand should be almost completely stationary except for clicking.

Repeat until that doesn't feel weird.

Replace the bowl with your dog, leaving the leash unclipped and hanging in the air for now and do the same exercise. Your dog will love this! Your left hand should be able to slide up and down the leash like a trombone while the right hand stays anchored at your torso. This will make more sense as we start practicing.

Now that you've practiced your leash-holding mechanics, put the leash away for the next few sections.

Lucky Lefts

I teach loose leash walking as a green light, yellow light, red light system. We're going to start with teaching the green light behavior because that's what you're going to use the most of by far.

You'll need your dog, your clicker and a full treat pouch—no leash necessary at this stage, so please start this skill inside or in a safely contained area, such as inside.

The first component of teaching loose leash walking is an exercise that I call "lucky lefts."

We're going to use the capturing skill you learned in the eye contact and sitting chapters at the beginning of the book. That's the one where you waited for the dog to make the correct decision on their own and then rewarded them for their independent choice, and then the dog learned how to be "stubbornly good" by repeatedly offering the correct behavior without prompting from you because it paid off in the past.

For this exercise, I want you to imagine an invisible bullseye about two feet in diameter floating directly beside your left knee. Any time that any part of your dog happens to be in that bullseye, click and treat. And when you're delivering the treat, place it right beside your left knee, even if your dog is veering wide or has already rushed past you.

This is deceptively simple but much more powerful than it appears.

First, you're capturing your dog's decision to be in the correct alignment with your body. Over time, this will basically turn you into a portable landmark to tell your dog where they should be in space no matter where you go. We're going to teach them that it rains cheese directly next to your left leg and there is a much lower chance of it raining cheese literally anywhere else on the planet. Smart dogs stay close to the cheese-leg!

And second, by delivering the food directly next to your leg instead of taking the treat to the dog, you're going to gradually "pull" the dog closer to you, which is going to make it easier to build this behavior in the long run. If they're expecting the treat to appear directly beside your knee, they're going to automatically stay closer to your knee, in the same way that a dog who has learned that the table produces food becomes very good at staying closer to the table at meal times. You can harness that behavior for the forces of good!

You'll still get there if you slip up and accidentally take the treat to the dog instead of requiring the dog to come to the treat. It happens to everybody sometimes—these rogue hands have a mind of their own! But you'll get there faster and more smoothly if you're consistent about paying as close to your body as you can.

If your dog is substantially taller or shorter than your knee, adjust accordingly, and when in doubt, deliver the food lower than where you think. You don't want the dog to be bouncing up on their tiptoes to get the treat or you're going to accidentally build in a jump, and that's no fun.

Take one step. If your dog is within a foot of your left leg, click and treat. While they're still chewing, take another step and as they catch up with your leg, click and treat. You want to almost "catch" them with the treat at your knee so that their mouth almost runs into your treat hand descending to give them their treat. Often, that means clicking when they're still a little bit behind you but approaching where you want them to be. This may take some practice.

Repeat this, taking one step at a time and clicking when the dog happens to be on your left side. It doesn't matter if the dog is in position on purpose or by accident at this point. If they rush ahead of you, make a 90 degree turn to the right and see if they re-orient to you and get back into the cheese zone—you can help them get back on track with some verbal encouragement if you want.

When you've got it right, this will start to take on a sort of dance-like feeling where you lead the dance by taking a step and your dog flows toward you by following your movement and catching up with your left leg.

If your dog is bumping at your treat hand or seems to be paying too much attention to the hand, I find it helpful to have my hand's home position just above my belly button, then drop my hand down to the outside of my knee to treat, then return my left hand to my stomach to make it visually clear to the dog whether a treat is available or not. If you're getting mouthing or jumping at all, definitely add this part, because it's likely that your dog thinks you're trying to lure them. It's a little more optional for small dogs and a little less optional for large dogs, but technically not required for either.

Building Duration

The next step is to build some duration to this component while working inside and off leash. Just like with the sits in the duration section, you're going to gradually increase the amount of time in between treats. With loose leash walking, it's usually easier to measure in steps rather than time elapsed. Start off paying every step like you were doing in the last section, but start to "forget" to click and treat the occasional step so your dog sometimes gets a treat every step and sometimes has to take two or three steps for one treat.

Gradually build up to taking more and more steps with your dog in the reward zone. If your dog disengages or gets lost somewhere in the process, help them get back on track by reducing the gap between treats on the next repetition and then continue on. For most dogs, this behavior builds momentum very quickly when you're practicing inside and off leash in a low-distraction area, so you can test your dog's limits a little bit more in this exercise than normal. This behavior becomes more difficult when you move outside where you're competing with a more interesting environment. Be prepared to pay more frequently in a more distracting environment, but you can usually stretch it quite a lot when you're practicing inside.

Once your dog is glued to your left leg when you're walking around inside, repeat the same exercise with the leash attached. As usual, you'll want to make it slightly easier in the beginning since we're changing an element, but dogs typically adjust to this step very quickly.

Lured Turns

When You Might Need Tight Turns

In most situations in day to day life, the average pet dog doesn't need especially pretty turns. I'm including this section because I also teach service dogs and dogs who will compete in sports someday and they will need to learn how to move their body more precisely in narrow areas. I personally teach this to my pet dogs too as a convenience skill, but you can consider this section optional if you don't mind your dog veering a bit wide on the turns overall. But if you're a completionist or want the extra experience points, it's a pretty easy set of exercises. We're going to teach your dog that the lucky lefts exercise above also applies to turns, which is a place where many dogs either overshoot (usually right turns) or get in the owner's way (usually left turns).

Luring Right Turns

For pretty much every dog on the planet who *isn't* mine, right turns are the easier direction. (I apparently raise exclusively goofy-footed dogs!) On a right turn, if your dog is on the left, you'll be taking the shorter path around the curve and your dog will be on the outside of the curve, which means they will be taking more steps and covering more distance to end up in the same place as you. Since dogs have more legs and tend to walk faster, this is usually a great bargain for them. For dogs who have naturally long stride lengths or a long history of rushing ahead of their owners, we start off on right loops when playing the lucky lefts game in the previous section to give them a teensy tiny advantage in the beginning to make use of this.

Like with most of the things in this book, we're going to separate out the behavior of turning, then incorporate it back into the walking behavior overall.

I like to practice this with my dog standing between me and a wall on my left, because it keeps them from swinging their butt a mile wide on the first turn, but that's optional. Start off with your dog on your left and roughly even with your left leg.

Click and give them a treat for beginning in the right position.

Prepare another treat in your left hand at your belly button. Step forward and turn 90 degrees to your right. While you are stepping, lower your left arm to lure your dog forward and into the reward zone beside your left leg.

Step forward and turn to the right again, luring the dog with you and releasing the treat into their mouth when they catch up to your left leg after you've finished moving.

Practice this until it feels fluid, then start mixing in some full 180 degree pivots without a pause in the middle in addition to the turns.

If your dog overshoots you and ends up passing the reward zone and ahead of you, just pivot again until they're a bit behind you on the circle and reward when they catch up to your leg again.

If your dog stays in place and doesn't move with you, use your voice to encourage them, bend slightly away from them at the waist and lure them back into the reward zone.

Start incorporating some straight steps too until it feels like a sort of large box-step with your dog as your dance partner.

Luring Left Turns

Left turns are definitely the harder direction for most dogs because on a tight left turn, the dog has to actually swing their butt behind you a little bit to pivot on their front legs while only their back legs move.

Dogs, bless them, do not come preloaded with a lot of awareness that they possess a back half. We make jokes about dogs who believe that they are floating heads, but honestly, it's a thing. If they haven't been taught to move their body carefully, most dogs are much more aware of their front legs' position than their rear legs' position, which is why this direction is harder.

For my competition dogs, I start teaching this with a platform pivot, but that is overkill for the majority of pet dogs that I work with. If you're interested enough to do it anyway, you can google how to use a pivot platform for heeling. For the rest of us, we're going to do the easy way with minimal prep work which ends in a less flashy turn, but also requires a lot less work to get there.

You'll need some sort of corner or edge. I love coffee tables for this, but wide doorways will work too. Have the dog between you and the barrier, with the corner about a step ahead of you and to the left.

Click and treat the dog for being to your left, then place another treat in front of their face as a lure. Step forward and wide around the corner to your left so that your body and the edge surface creates a sort of channel for your dog, like bumpers on both sides of a bowling lane. You should be stepping in an L shape with the forward step being the shorter line of the L, then a 90 degree turn to the left, then the longer part of the L with your dog on the inside of the turn. When your dog catches up to your left leg and the treat hand, release the treat into their mouth.

If you're able to feed from the far side of their face with your hand alongside the left side of their muzzle, as if you were trying to put the treat into their left canine teeth, you can get a much tighter turn.

Step Back Reset

Teaching a Yellow Light

I said in the beginning that we were going to teach loose leash walking as a green light, yellow light, red light system. We've already worked on the green light portion, which is the lucky lefts exercise in the previous exercise. That's what to do while your dog is moving with you and keeping the leash loose by your left leg.

Now we're going to install your yellow light behavior, which is what you'll use if your dog is moving slightly ahead of you or has disconnected from you to engage with a distraction in the environment but there's still a brain in the skull.

I think of this as a sort of "check yourself before you wreck yourself" skill to remind the dog how to get back on the right track after a lapse. You'd be amazed how many dogs completely lose focus after an absolutely tiny error because they learned how to *be* in the loose leash walking zone but they never learned how to *get back there*. So, we're going to teach them how to get there.

As with before, you'll be training this inside and off leash with the clicker in your right hand and your left hand free for treating the dog.

Start off with your dog in front of you, which is where they're most likely to be when they forget that they were supposed to be walking politely on a loose leash or get distracted by something in the world. Have a treat in your left hand.

Keeping your right foot planted facing forward, turn your body and pivot backward (or counterclockwise) with your left foot so that your feet are facing in opposite directions. If you imagine your position as a clock's face, if you started off facing 12:00, you're now facing 9:00 with your left foot pointing toward 6:00 and your right foot still pointing toward 12:00.

Next, draw a line with your left treat hand from your dog (at 12:00, what used to be in front of you) to where your left foot is pointing (at 6:00, what used to be behind you) as if to say, "Hey *you,* go over *here.*"

The end position should look a little bit like you are doing a jumping jack—left arm outstretched to point, left foot pointing the same direction, right foot exactly where it started.

Next, shift your weight onto your left leg as if you were going to step in that direction.

You basically want your entire body language to say "I am going THIS WAY" in capital letters, including a lure to bring your dog to the 6:00 position. If your dog stares at you like you've lost your mind, tilt your shoulders and torso toward your left hand and give your dog a couple of seconds to think about it. Yes, this often looks absolutely ridiculous the first few times you try it, but I promise it gets *much* more fluid with some practice.

When your dog reaches your pointing left hand, give them one treat at 6:00 and then bring your left foot back to the starting position and your left hand back to neutral, giving your dog a second treat when they catch up with your left leg facing the correct direction.

Your dog should have gone from standing in front position to walking behind you, turning around and should now be standing in heel position oriented the same way you are. They should have gotten a treat at the furthest back point and a second treat when returning to heel position.

This feels incredibly awkward the first dozen or so times you do it, but will get drastically smoother with practice. It helps to practice without the dog a little bit so the movement is smooth before you add the dog.

To start the next repetition, toss a treat a few feet ahead of you to simulate your dog pulling ahead out of heel position, then begin again when your dog reorients to you at front position.

The nice thing about this is that for about 95% of dogs, this skill comes pretty much pre-loaded and if your body language is doing the right thing, the dog is going to do the right thing too. The downside is that it looks a bit silly in the short term until you've built up the muscle memory to do the whole movement fluidly.

Practice this behavior until you're able to fade down the hand sign to something more subtle—mine is a rock back onto the left leg and a quick gesture behind me with the left arm. You can fade out the treat at the furthest back point and just treat when the dog returns to heel position.

Seen from above, the dog should be making a large 6 shape or paperclip shape, with the top part of the 6 beginning in front of you, looping around behind you to the left and then closing the loop by returning to heel position.

Once this feels comfortable, start incorporating it into your lucky lefts routine off leash and inside. While your dog is on the left, do lucky lefts as before. If your dog starts to leave the reward zone to move ahead of you, take a quick step back with your left leg to help lure them behind you on the left side, reward them for returning to heel and start moving forward again, switching back to lucky lefts. When your dog has mastered that step, add the leash while practicing inside.

Circle Method Reset

Red Light: When to Circle

We've covered our green light and our yellow light skills already. Next up is our red light behavior, which we are going to use sparingly and only when neither the green light nor the yellow light have worked on their own. This method comes to us via Denise Fenzi, although the way I teach it is a variation on her method rather than the original.

If we're doing loose leash walking perfectly, we never have to use the red light under normal circumstances because we've done such a good job picking our practice areas and rewarding our dog for the correct behavior that there's never a genuine need to physically manage them when they're pulling.

Unfortunately, the perfect world and the real world are rarely the same, so this is an error-management system for those shit-hits-the-fan moments when you just need to keep the dog out of traffic or when you can't be in trainer-mode but your dog needs to go somewhere on leash.

I use the circle method when the dog has completely blown out of the green light zone and is either too distracted or too far ahead of me to use the step back reset that we worked on in the yellow light section—the "SQUIRREL!" moments. The yellow light reset is for small but potentially frequent errors. The red light reset is for "Oh god, he's seen a running rabbit and I need him to not drag me into the road." It gives you a mechanical advantage over the dog to make it harder for him to pull you, but it doesn't replace training.

What the Circle Method Looks Like

The circle method, like martial arts, uses your dog's own force against them in a way that prevents them from having physical leverage over you.

When a dog pulls on the leash, the leash is typically aligned parallel with the spine and the dog is able to throw their entire weight against the leash without disrupting their center of gravity. They can spread their shoulders and haul forward like a freight train, which can be dangerous if your dog is substantially larger or stronger than you are. The circle method moves the dog slightly off balance, which interrupts their ability to hunker down and haul forward.

Think of your dog's ability to pull as being similar to a crocodile's jaw. According to Google, a crocodile has a bite strength of about 3,500 pounds per square inch—in other words, if they want to close their mouth, it's *gonna* close, because their entire body design prioritizes jaw closing strength. But the muscles that they use to open their jaws are comparatively weak—so weak that you can hold a croc's mouth closed with your bare hands or some duct tape.

(Footnote: I know we talked about citizen scientists earlier in the book, but please do not test this assertion at home. Author not responsible for curious readers consumed by reptiles.)

Which means that if you're trying to control a crocodile's jaw, you are going to have *vastly* different experiences depending on whether you are trying to hold it open or hold it closed. Using the same amount of pressure on the same body part in different directions can give dramatically different outcomes.

A dog's ability to pull is similar. Dog's bodies are great at moving forward and backward, but they have almost no pulling power laterally to the side or in an arc. By redirecting their forward pulling into circular pulling on an arc, you are giving yourself the mechanical advantage—essentially changing the task from holding the croc's mouth open to holding the croc's mouth shut.

A front attach harness works similarly to redirect a dog back toward the handler when they begin to pull and for some dogs, this may be a better option.

When your dog pulls ahead of you, the clip on the leash is moved to the back of their neck, aligned with the spine at twelve o'clock. Slide your left hand down the leash to act as a rudder and rotate the angle of the leash so that the clip is on the side of the dog's neck instead, aligned with the bottom of their right ear at three o'clock. At the same time, begin to step in a small circle to the right, keeping your left hip toward your dog. Most dogs will curve their path of travel to yield into the leash. Instead of pulling forward in a straight line, they pull in an arc or clockwise circle around you. This drastically reduces the amount of pulling power they can exert.

If they continue to pull outward, turn them gently in a broad clockwise circle around you, like lunging a horse. If the dog is leaning outward toward the distractions, they will continue to go in a circle around you instead of forward for as long as the leash is attached to the side of their neck rather than the back.

You should turn with your dog so that they are essentially a satellite orbiting you in heel position—they should stay aligned with your left hip.

As soon as they release the tension from the leash or turn their head toward the midline or inside of the circle (rather than leaning forward or outward), give them a treat for returning to heel position and continue forward using your green light behavior.

And make sure that *you* aren't holding pressure on the leash or else you won't be able to feel it when your dog stops pulling—which can be hard if you have a lot of experience with walking a canine freight train in the past and your body is automatically braced for impact. This method works best if the line between pressure and no-pressure is very clear to both parties.

The circling prevents your dog from physically dragging you toward the distraction that they were trying to access, which also prevents them from paying themselves for pulling, which removes a lot of the incentive to pull if they know that putting pressure on the leash does not lead to being able to approach the object of their heart's desire.

Many people have learned to "be a tree" when their dog pulls, which does work, but it can be *extremely* frustrating in the early steps with a dog who just wants to *go*, and it requires an astronomical amount of patience from the person in the beginning stages, especially with a boisterous large breed dog. The circle method, by contrast, allows the dog to keep moving so they are less frustrated by the stop-and-start of errors ("charge forward! brakes! charge forward! brakes!"), but still prevents them from accessing the reinforcer. It also teaches them to be conscious of their own leash pressure.

If you're experiencing dizziness, it helps to walk in a small circle on the inside of your dog's circle rather than pivoting neatly on a point. Instead of looking directly outward at your dog (with your gaze straight out from the center like a clock's hand), it helps to look forward on your path of travel around your own tiny circle (as if you were marching forward in a one-foot-diameter circle).

If my dog is walking politely on the leash, I don't mind approaching dog-safe distractions at all—those are great reinforcers for good behavior, as long as you can make access to them contingent on polite walking. My dogs are welcome to pee on the fire hydrant, sniff that bush, check out the ducks in the pond across the park, be my guest. Walks are for my dogs as much as for me, so as long as my dogs are walking politely, I'm perfectly happy to go where they want to go plenty of the time (within reason, obviously—we're not walking into traffic or into the neighbor's yard no matter how much my dog wants to).

But at the point when the leash goes tight, my dog loses my permission to steer our walks. If you misplace your brain and pull, we're going in a clockwise circle. If you can walk politely, you have the keys to the kingdom. Choose wisely.

5

Dog Meet World

Leashes and Thresholds

Working with Distractions on Leash

So far, you've been working on your leash manners in low distraction environments as much as possible. But as I'm sure you've grumbled under your breath a time or two while reading these instructions, the real world has distractions and your dog is going to need to learn how to cope around interesting things in the environment that they aren't able to access. Whether it's a dead bird on the sidewalk, another dog they can't greet or a pond they would dearly love to swim in, sometimes dogs don't get what they want, and that can be a challenge for their loose leash walking behaviors when they have big feelings about the distractions in the world.

It's worth noting that the more work you do on teaching your leash manners in a low-distraction environment, the less work you'll have to do to manage your dog around distractions *by far*. Distractions are tricky to work through, but the more mileage you can put onto making loose leash walking the obvious autopilot behavior, the less work you'll have to do when you're trying to get your dog past their ten-out-of-ten, brain-has-exploded, cannot-function, top-shelf distraction, whatever that happens to be for your individual dog.

Or in other words, the more well-paved the road to the correct behavior is, the easier it will be to get them back on track when they're struggling.

"Tame" Distractions and "Wild" Distractions

As mentioned previously, when I'm working with distractions, I like to mentally categorize them as "wild" distractions and "tame" distractions. As far as I know, I'm the only person who uses that terminology, but the distinction makes sense to me and I hope it will make sense to you too.

Wild distractions are things that are out in the world, usually with moving parts or with spatial constraints that make them very difficult to avoid, ignore or navigate. They're the things that just crop up in the middle of your life and make you deal with them—how rude. If you're complaining about how distractible your dog is, you're almost definitely talking about how much they struggle with wild distractions.

Tame distractions, on the other hand, have been domesticated. They're under your control and can be used for your purposes. That makes them fabulous assets for training. For me, tame distractions are usually things that I've intentionally set up as training opportunities for my dog, or wild distractions that I can manage well enough that I can functionally use them and I am very confident that I can easily control whether my dog accesses the distraction or not.

As much as you possibly can, you want to prioritize working with tame distractions when you are trying to build your dog's skills.

That means food that you've intentionally planted for your dog to notice and leave alone, or distractions on the opposite side of a fence, or something that you can spot from more than a leash's length away so you can prevent your dog from self-reinforcing with it.

Rule of thumb: practice with tame distractions, navigate around wild distractions when possible.

When you come across a distraction in your training, especially when you're out on a walk, ask yourself whether this is a tame or a wild distraction. Can you use distance, a barrier or a leash to completely control your dog's access to the distraction so they can't pay themself for making an error? Can you control how tempting the distraction is for your dog or is the distract-o-meter stuck at a ten-out-of-ten? Does the value of the distraction outweigh the value of the reinforcers you have available to use?

Many of my students are surprised to learn that I *don't* suggest accepting every training challenge the world throws at you. If your German shorthaired pointer is a newbie at polite leash walking and there's a whole flock of geese on your normal walking path, that is a boss-battle-level distraction compared to your dog's skill level. If you walk right up to those geese and try to train through it, you are very unlikely to leave that training session feeling satisfied because your dog is almost certain to make an error (and pay themself handsomely for doing so). Relative to your dog's skill level, that distraction is too wild.

But on leash and at a distance from the geese? Far enough away that your dog is only moderately interested but still has enough brain to stay connected with you? That's a *much* tamer distraction and you are *much* more likely to make training progress with an appropriate level of distraction.

And the cool thing is that as your dog's skills level up, they can handle wilder and wilder distractions.

For example, I live with a house full of high-octane herdy dogs. On the first day of training, when we haven't put any work into domesticating their distractions yet, my dogs would choose chasing other animals over pretty much any type of reinforcer I can offer and they wouldn't even have to think about it. But because we've successfully practiced working around many, *many* tame distractions where I could reinforce my dogs for making the right decisions (and prevent them from making the wrong ones) while my dogs leveled up their skills, I can now easily call my off-leash dogs away from a herd of bolting deer when the dogs are an acre or two away from me, even if I have no treats available.

In other words, practicing with tame distractions allowed me to build up to working with wild ones once my dogs had enough experience points to make the right decisions.

So when we're working with distractions, the goal is not to find the biggest, toughest distraction available and conquer it on day one to prove that you can. That is almost certain to backfire, which is almost certain to reward your dog for doing exactly the opposite of what you want them to do.

But by beginning with predictable, controllable tame distractions at your dog's skill level, you can give them the opportunity to grow *without* simultaneously giving them a chance to practice making errors. These controlled setups allow you to keep the difficulty level in the sweet spot where your dog can work hard but get it right.

Yo-Yo Leave It Practice

One of my favorite games to practice with a tame distraction is what I call the yo-yo leave it game, because your dog is going to feel like a canine yo-yo being drawn toward the distraction and then back toward you.

Plant a distraction in a low-traffic, low-distraction area at least ten feet away from any barriers that you are going to have to navigate (e.g., don't put it at the bottom of your apartment stairs where the dog is going to have to almost trip over it to get to the training area). Driveways are awesome for this—I like to put the distraction right in the middle if

I can. A cheap bowl with a handful of dog kibble works well. I try not to use especially smelly treats for this, both to make the exercise easier for my inexperienced dog and to minimize the chance of beckoning the hoards of ants lying in wait for a picnic.

Using your loose leash walking skills, walk toward the distraction and notice the point when your dog sees the bowl of treats but *before* they pull forward to get to it and *before* they are within leash range of the bowl. As soon as your dog sees the distraction, *stop*. Plant your feet. If they haven't seen the bowl when you're ten feet away from the distraction, go farther away from the bowl and then re-approach until they notice it, but most dogs will notice it on the first try (because duh, it's a bowl full of dinner sitting out there in the world and obviously waiting to be eaten by a dog, says the opportunistic scavenger species).

If your dog is straining on the leash or scrabbling to get toward the distraction, use your red light circle method to spiral your dog away from the distraction of the bowl. Move another ten feet away from the distraction and plant your feet again. If your dog is still trying to drag you toward the distraction, move farther away again and keep spiraling or circling until the dog stops with their feet planted and looking at the distraction without hauling on the leash.

Once your dog is firmly planted with all four feet and looking at the distraction, keeping your leash in the same place so that it does not increase the pressure on the leash, take a step backward with your left foot like the step back reset and lean your weight onto your left leg. Your hand should stay fixed in space where it is, but your body should move away from your hand, while you extend your arm to compensate. To me, this motion feels a little bit like my leash hand is a hinge and my body is a door opening away from my dog. The hinge doesn't move; the door does.

Nine times out of ten, the dog is going to turn their head back toward you to see what you're doing. Perfect! Click and treat by your left leg, return your leg to neutral position. Then allow them to re-focus on the distraction and use your step back to prompt them to turn away from the distraction again, clicking the moment that they decide to stop staring at the distraction and see what you're doing instead.

The place where the dog is able to stand with all four feet planted but still visibly interested in the distraction is called the threshold. To oversimplify, this is the line between where they can ignore the distraction and where they can't. If you move closer to the distraction, your dog will be over threshold, which means that their judgment will be impaired and they will be likely to make errors, such as pulling to strain toward the distraction. If you move farther away from the distraction, your dog will be under threshold, which means that they will be operating rationally and not feeling as emotional about the distraction. For this exercise, you want to be working *on* their threshold or slightly under—always err on the side of under if you're unsure.

After ten repetitions, you should be building a sort of yo-yo pattern where the dog looks or leans toward the distraction, then self-interrupts and checks back in with you for a click and a treat before looking at the distraction again. Let them refocus on the distraction at will as long as they're not straining toward it or making a fool of themself, and as long as there's no risk that they're going to get to the distraction.

This is a variation on Leslie McDevitt's Look At That game. The more fluent your dog becomes with seeing a distraction and checking back in with you, the easier it will be to build the distractions themselves into cues to check in with you, and the easier it will be for you to domesticate the wild distractions in your life.

If you are working at or below threshold, the more times you pay your dog for voluntarily looking away from the distraction, the more value you build for checking in with you and the tamer the distraction will become.

Management

An Ounce of Prevention is Worth a Pound of Cure

You may notice that a theme of the above section is generally that preventing access to the problematic thing is a viable way to save yourself a lot of work. In dog training as in most things, an ounce of prevention is worth a pound of cure and if it's possible to just avoid the problem situation entirely, that is a perfectly legitimate choice to make.

It takes much less work to teach a dog to walk politely on a leash if they've never learned that pulling gets them closer to the things they want to access.

It takes much less work to teach a dog to stand calmly for greetings if they've never been allowed to leap gleefully all over the guests or rush up to total strangers on the street to tackle them with love.

It takes much less work to convince a dog that something isn't scary if you're starting from neutral rather than from already scared.

The more errors you can prevent by preemptively managing your dog's environment, the less training you will have to do in the long run and the easier your life with your dog will be. Everything the world throws at you does not have to be a training moment, especially if you know that your dog doesn't (yet) have the skills to get it right. You can build those skills in non-emergency situations. It is completely acceptable to opt out, manage around, prevent, minimize and patch through when necessary to get the job done.

Are You in Trainer Mode? If Not, Then Manage

The question to ask yourself is, "Am I in trainer mode right now?"

If you're in trainer mode, then you are actively working on improving the way your dog interacts with the environment. You're focused on the dog side of the equation and you're going to do what it takes to set your dog up to make the right choices, then reinforce those choices so your dog is likely to repeat them again in the future. You have deliberately set the challenge at a level where your dog can succeed and you are confident that your dog will make the right decision *without* paying themself for an error first.

The more time you can spend in trainer mode, the better trained your dog will ultimately be and the faster they'll get there, for obvious reasons.

If, on the other hand, you just need to move from point A to point B and you really don't have time to be fussy about how it happens, switch over to management mode.

In management mode, you're focused less on how you can teach the dog the correct behavior and more on how you can adjust the situation to make the requirements for your dog lower this one time. For example, if you have a small breed dog and you need to walk them from your car to the vet's office but you know that they're going to pull you into the clinic and you don't want them to practice pulling, carry them the twenty feet into the office. If you have company coming over in two minutes and you don't have time to work with the dog's jumping as the guests come in and you're worried the dog will make an error (and that the guests may reinforce them for it, "Oh, I don't mind"), you're allowed to crate the dog or have them in another room with a chew so they aren't practicing impolite greeting behavior. It's better to avoid the situation than to put more mileage on a problem behavior you're trying to erase or replace.

And then, of course, make a note about the situation where you needed to lean on management, because that will be your lesson plan for the next training session.

All other things being equal, it seems like people naturally polarize to one side of the management issue or the other. Either they pitch the puppy into the deep end and hope they can swim or they get stuck in management mode forever without ever addressing the issue with training.

There's a middle ground here, folks, and the middle ground is firmly where you want to be in most cases.

In the short term, manage around the issue without shame. Prioritize preventing errors. If you're in a tight spot and you can't be in trainer mode, then do what you gotta do to get through the situation with management for damage-control.

But when you're *not* in a tight spot anymore, make sure you put some work into those skills so you don't have to lean as heavily on management the next time. Can you replicate the situation without the time pressure, such as working on walking your dog into the vet clinic when you *don't* have an appointment, maybe when the vet staff is on lunch break? Can you ask a friend to be your very patient, very boring "guest" for some door manners work next weekend? Ask yourself what part of the situation was the most challenging for your dog, break that part down into its easiest units and start to chip away at it incrementally so your dog can handle more responsibility next time.

Environmental Cues

What Are Environmental Cues?

We've talked about attaching verbal and hand sign cues earlier in the book, but I wanted to take this opportunity to talk about a third kind of cue that you can use to level up your dog training: environmental cues.

Environmental cues are anything out in the world that prompts a behavior from your dog or tips them off about what behavior is going to be reinforcable next. For most dogs, a leash is an environmental cue that going to the door will be reinforced by a walk. Many people have taught their dog that a full food bowl is a cue to sit and wait calmly as the bowl is lowered to the ground. This is a great start, but you can get incredibly geeky with environmental cues to build helpful default behaviors for your dog.

I do a reasonable amount of service dog training and environmental cues are *hugely* beneficial in the service dog world. My service dog needs to know that a checkout line means to settle beside me, a dining table means to curl up under the table and expect to stay there, their vest means that they are in service dog mode and can't acknowledge the people around them, the end of an aisle means pause for me to make sure we're not going to run into anyone, a shopping cart means heel slightly farther back than usual, and so on. Service dogs need to be able to "autopilot" in a wide variety of environments without constant micromanagement from their handler, so we lean on environmental cues a *lot*.

But environmental cues are awesome for working with pet dogs too, because the more information your dog can get from the environment, the less active steering you need to do to keep them on the right track. A solid repertoire of environmental cues is as close as you can get to a canine autopilot.

And the good news is that these cues are not even particularly tricky to teach! In fact, I bet your dog already knows a few. Here are a few examples of environmental cues that many dogs pick up on their own:

Hear a doorbell ring (or a car in the driveway) -> bark like crazy

Human stands up -> check in to see if we're about to do something fun

It's 5:30 pm -> wait at the door for owner to come home

Human touches leash -> rush to the door

Human stops walking -> pause on a walk

Car door opens -> jump into car

In each of those cases, the natural consequence that follows after the dog's behavior is reinforcing your dog's choice. If the car door opens and your dog jumps in, there is an above-average chance that they are going to get to take a ride somewhere interesting. This is useful to know if you would like to substitute a different behavior into the recipe. You can keep the same cue and reinforcer, but switch out the behavior in the middle.

For example, let's say that your dog goes nuts every time a guest rings the doorbell and you would prefer a less vocal greeting. If the behavior has become habitual, that is a huge clue that there is a reinforcer at the end of the sequence somewhere—which means that if you can find that pot of gold at the end of the rainbow, you can use it to reinforce a different behavior instead. In the case of a dog who barks (happily) when guests arrive, the reinforcer is likely social attention from your guests. Knowing that, you can manipulate access to that social reinforcement so it pays for a behavior you'd prefer. You could have a friend ring your doorbell and ask them to just wait on your porch for a minute while you cue your dog to go to their mat and lie down. As soon as your dog lies down on their mat, signal your guest to come in and allow your dog to greet. With successful repetition, your dog will hear the doorbell and head for their mat to settle.

Sit at Doorways

One of the most common environmental cues I teach to client dogs is to sit at exterior doorways before being released to go outside. This keeps your dog out of traffic and keeps them stationary while you put the leash on if you don't have a fenced yard. If you do have a fenced yard, requiring it anyway is one extra practice repetition of a sit stay to build that "muscle" and a nice way to build up their impulse control.

And as a bonus, it's dead simple to teach. Ready?

Every time you get ready to open the door, ask the dog to sit before you open the door.

Yes, it's actually that simple! For the vast majority of dogs, the opportunity to go outside is valuable and something they're very willing to sit for. A five-second sit for a thirty-minute walk is a heck of a bargain! Ask for a sit when you touch the exterior door's doorknob every time and you will quickly have a dog who plants their butt at the door when they want to go outside.

You are essentially creating a tiny behavior chain. A **behavior chain** is a series of behaviors connected together with each link in the chain reinforcing the previous link. In this case, you are **backchaining** because you are starting with the strongest part of the chain (the part they have practiced a lot, going for a walk) at the end of the sequence and then adding new behaviors to the front of the chain. For our purposes, backchaining is usually the most effective way to chain behaviors because the dog is always moving from newer skills to the more familiar or more reinforcing part of the chain.

If you cue "sit" every time you touch the doorknob to the outside door, your dog will start to recognize the pattern and cut corners. If the doorknob *always* means sit, then there's no reason to wait for you to say the word "sit." Touching the doorknob becomes enough of a clue that a sit will pay off. Once you see this connection starting to form, you can start introducing a pause after touching the doorknob to give the door an opportunity to offer a sit, which you can then reinforce with the walk. With repetition, as soon as you touch the door, your dog will plant their butt in a sit and wait politely to be let outside without you having to say a word.

For very boisterous dogs, I'll add in a stay component where they need to stay sitting even with the door wide open. Start off barely opening the door a crack, click/treat for remaining sitting. Open a crack farther, click/treat for remaining sitting. If your dog stands up or breaks their stay, block them from exiting, close the door before they can go through and go back to an easier step on the next repetition. When they've held their stay successfully for several seconds with the door open, give your release cue, pay them one more time as you go through the doorway and begin the walk. With consistency, this builds into an automatic wait at doorways until released, which is much more pleasant than being gleefully dragged over the threshold while you try to get your keys, poop bags and leash all sorted out.

Sit for the Leash

If you've taught your dog to sit for their food bowl to be lowered, you can use the exact same method to teach your dog to sit while you put their leash on them. Ask the dog to sit; click and treat. Move the leash toward the collar; click and treat if they're still sitting. Touch the collar with the leash snap; click and treat for sitting. Touch the collar with the open leash snap; click and treat. Leash the dog; click and treat. Unleash the dog; click and treat. Repeat until your dog automatically sits as soon as they see the leash come out and stays stationary while you get the clasp hooked onto their collar. No more wrestling with a wiggling, excited dog!

If they leave their sit, that's fine—but leashes doesn't move closer to collars on standing dogs.

For most dogs, the leash is a highly desirable part of their day because it means they're about to go on a walk and see the world. If you make that reinforcer contingent on sitting while the leash is being put on, you'll have a dog who automatically sits for the leash in no time. It's the little things, you know?

Voicemail Behavior

I also like to teach dogs a category of behaviors that I call voicemail behaviors. These are human behaviors that can signal to your dog, "Owner is not home right now. Please leave a message and we will return your call at our earliest convenience." In other words, it's a type of ongoing signal that you will not be providing any additional reinforcement opportunities for the duration of this cue, so they shouldn't bother asking.

For example, I do a lot of work on my laptop and I have several large, energetic, high-maintenance herdy dogs. From very early in their life, they learn that if my laptop is in my lap, "Mom is not home right now" and I will not be responsive to non-emergency needs. If they drop a toy on my laptop, I will put the toy in my pocket and keep answering emails. If they whine that they want to go on a walk, they will be ignored. As a result, by about six months old, pretty much every dog that comes through my house learns that my laptop in my lap is an environmental cue to go lie down and entertain themself quietly while I work—and I don't have to say a thing. The presence of my laptop in my lap is a cue that means reinforcement is not available right now. And on the flip side, closing my laptop has become a sort of release cue, like "Oh boy, Mom's home again!" even though I have been sitting in front of them the whole time.

Whether you know it or not, you probably have some equivalent of this and you can intentionally cultivate more if you'd like. The key here is to be very clear about what begins the voicemail condition, what ends it and what needs override it. If you sometimes respond to the dogs and sometimes don't, you're essentially training them to get more and more efficient at interrupting you (because they are reinforced under the conditions where you respond to them and not when you don't, and behavior follows reinforcement). You absolutely do not want to accidentally shape your dog to be a master at interrupting you more efficiently!

If you want to teach a voicemail behavior, here are the criteria you need to meet before beginning:

Are the dog's biological needs being met? (Empty-ish bladder, water available, not in distress, etc.)

Will the dog's biological needs still be met for the duration of the voicemail period? (For example, am I asking the dog to be ignored for longer than they can hold their bladder without discomfort?)

Is there a single clear cue that tells the dog when I become unavailable to respond to dog needs? (In most cases, this is an environmental cue such as the presence of a laptop, talking on the phone, sitting down to eat and so on, but it can also be a verbal cue such as "Take a break.")

Is there a single clear cue that tells the dog when I become available to respond to dog needs again?

Under what conditions will I respond to my dog even during voicemail time? (For example, I will respond to my dog if they make "I'm about to vomit" noises, if any dog indicates pain or physical distress, to prevent the puppy from pestering the older dogs or if my service dog alerts.) Knowing what will count as an override ahead of time makes it much easier to maintain clear boundaries.

Can I safely ignore the types of behaviors my dog is likely to offer during this time if my dog does try to "leave a voicemail"? For example, if I am working with a young puppy, I may or may not be able to safely ignore the behavior that they offer. Maybe I'm in a puppy-proofed room where they really do not have access to anything that would prompt an undesirable behavior and they're solid enough on potty training that I'm not stressing it. Great! That's a good candidate for voicemail behavior time. But if I still need to watch them like a hawk to potty train them or if they periodically chew that one spot on the carpet and I can't let that keep happening, then I am going to need to respond to my dog even when I intend to ignore them if they initiate those behaviors, which will degrade my voicemail settle behavior. In a situation where I know I will be tempted to respond to my dog, I may put them in a crate with a chew instead so I can completely prevent them from doing behavior that I would need to redirect or respond to.

Fading Reinforcement

Moving to Life Rewards

By this point in the book, your dog has picked up a wide repertoire of new skills and you have become an expert at reinforcing them for their good decisions (and preventing reinforcement for the questionable ones too).

If you're like most of my clients, the next question on your mind is, "When can I stop using so much food?"

First, let me say that I don't think there's a single thing wrong with continuing to use food to reinforce behaviors indefinitely as long as you haven't gotten yourself into a bribery situation.

Personally, I'm happy to keep a few treats in my pocket to pay for behavior that is convenient to me. It takes virtually no effort from me, I enjoy sharing pleasant things with my dogs and it keeps their behaviors nice and strong.

I think the majority of people who are in a big rush to get rid of the food at all costs are likely falling into the show-me-the-money trap and worry that their dog's obedience immediately ends when the last treat crumb in their pocket is gone. And I hate to break it to you, but that's not a problem with using food; that's user error. If that made you feel a little twinge of, "Yikes, that might be me," reviewing the chapter on fading lures will get you sorted out!

But let's say you're not talking about getting rid of all reinforcement forever—you just want to know when you can taper down to a more realistic long-term level so you don't feel like you're a walking pez dispenser for your pup.

To answer that, let's talk about what happens to behavior over time.

In a nutshell, behavior is not static. It's always either improving or degrading, even if only by tiny amounts.

Sometimes, I like to think of the strength of behaviors like the cleanliness of my kitchen. No matter how hard I try to tidy up after myself at every step throughout the day, my kitchen is in a constant state of either getting dirtier or getting cleaner. There's never a point when I can clean my kitchen "once and for all" so I have a "fully cleaned kitchen" and then "stop using cleaning." Without upkeep, it would rapidly degrade into a mess just as a side effect of living in that space. Every interaction that I have with my kitchen is either moving it toward a slightly-cleaner kitchen or a slightly-dirtier kitchen—and the more I use it, the more often I need to clean it, because using a kitchen inherently creates some amount of mess.

Behavior is kind of like that. Every time you cue a behavior, it's either getting a little bit stronger (if it achieves a desirable consequence) or a little bit weaker (if it doesn't). Those consequences accumulate over time, either snowballing into a big fat reinforcement history ("Oh yeah, this *definitely* works!") or dwindling into obscurity ("I thought there was a pattern here, but I guess not").

So if we want to decrease the food to a more sustainable long-term level but we also don't want our behaviors to degrade over time, how do we taper down on the food in a way that keeps our behaviors nice and strong?

We start building in a whole buffet of other desirable things that we

FADING REINFORCEMENT

can give our dogs instead of or in addition to food.

A lot of the behaviors that we've worked on in this book come with their eventual reinforcers pre-installed. In most cases, we're not teaching a totally stand-alone behavior without context—we're teaching a more polite behavior to access the same reinforcer that they have already been seeking. After all, most of the unwanted behaviors that we are trying to resolve in dog training were previously paid handsomely by their natural consequences—and those reinforcers were potent enough to build reliable (if undesirable) behaviors. That means all we have to do is pull a switcheroo in the middle so the dog performs a different behavior in the same context to access the same reinforcer and then we end up with a behavior almost on autopilot.

For example, sitting politely before going through the front door is reinforced by access to the yard or a walk—the same reinforcer that was previously maintaining the default "rush through the door" behavior. We start off by using a cookie so that the new behavior (sitting politely) can out-compete the old behavior (rushing through the door), but once the behavior is solid, we can fade down the cookies and continue to reinforce the behavior by opening the door contingent on the dog sitting politely.

Similarly, you reinforce polite greeting skills by allowing your dog to greet when they're being polite and by preventing them from using rude behavior to access attention successfully. You maintain good leash manners because tight leashes never go anywhere interesting and pulling doesn't get your dog where they want to go anymore. Those rewards are built into the behavior.

Those are the easy ones. We use food as a bonus reinforcer to get the behavior started, but the long term reinforcer is "you get to access that thing you already wanted."

For other behaviors where there is no reward built into the behavior, like stay, recall and leave it, you can layer in a variety of life rewards *and* continue to pay intermittently with food or other reinforcers. Sometimes, a stay will result in a cookie. Sometimes it results in permission to go play with their dog-friends. Sometimes you release them from the stay and throw the ball.

And what about the clicker?

The clicker is a precision tool used for pinpointing the exact moment of the behavior which earned your dog a reward. It is primarily used to build or improve behavior. Once you reach maintenance, you can retire your clicker to a drawer somewhere until the next time you want to teach something new.

There's a common misconception that the click will eventually be used as a substitute treat and that you will be able to click as the entire reward rather than paying your dog. Bluntly: This is bad training and it is absolutely guaranteed to fail (and usually quickly). The entire power of the click lies in its ability to predict that The Good Stuff is about to happen to your dog. If you break that pairing by repeatedly clicking without producing The Good Stuff, you are weakening the power of your clicker.

Instead, fade the clicker out of the picture but continue to reward the behavior with access to something your dog likes, whether that is food, attention, walks, toys, praise, greeting strangers, sniffing a fire hydrant, or anything else they find desirable.

As you're starting to move away from a 1:1 behavior-to-food-reward ratio, it can be helpful to start stashing food rewards in dog-safe places around your house, such as on top of a bookcase or in a drawer that your dog can't get into. Cue an easy behavior in a situation where your dog can see that you have no cookies in your pocket. When they do the behavior, rush to the treat stash immediately for their reward. Using this method, you can build up their faith that even if you don't have The Good Stuff immediately available, you always have access to it and it is always worth responding to known cues, even if it doesn't look like a training session.

Behavioral Bank Accounts and Canine Credit Scores

If you read a lot of dog training books, you'll see a common metaphor that compares your dog's behavior to a bank account.

In that metaphor, every time you reinforce your dog for doing a behavior, you're paying into the bank account for that behavior. Every time you ask them to do the behavior without reinforcement, you're taking a withdrawal from the bank account, which you can do without penalty as long as you've made enough payments in.

I do not love this metaphor.

Instead, I prefer to think of it as a credit score, which is a little more complex and a lot more accurate.

Every time you cue a behavior, you are placing that behavior on credit, because you are getting the part you want up front before you show them the money. If a cue is a signal that reinforcement is available contingent on a behavior, then the cue is functionally a way of saying "Trust me, pup: I'm good for it." And training is the process of proving that.

Your dog gives you the behavior on credit with the expectation that it will come back to them in the form of reinforcement.

If you reinforce your dog, you are paying off your credit card on time and in full. Over time, a history of reliable payment improves your canine credit score, which means your dog may be willing to give you more of a "credit line" of behavior before they need to see the money.

Sometimes, you have to carry a balance. You ask for a behavior and you can't pay for it immediately. That's fine—that's one of the functions of credit. We've spent all this time teaching your dog to respond to cues so that we *don't* have to show them the money before they do the behavior. Sometimes, you ask for a behavior when you have no access to meaningful reinforcement, and if your credit score is good, your dog will give you the behavior up front anyway and you go on with your life.

But that debt doesn't disappear. Now your canine credit line is carrying a balance. The larger that balance is and the longer you carry it without repaying it, the more your canine credit score is going to decay.

If you practice the same skill in situations where you *can* reinforce it, you can pay down that balance and maintain your good credit—and even improve it by proving that you are a safe gamble.

But if you continue to ask for behaviors and routinely make charges to that account without repaying, your credit score will get dinged. If you have a history of missed payments, eventually your dog is going to run a credit check when you ask for a behavior and they're going to say, "You've proven that you're not good for it."

Practicing your dog's known skills with reinforcement is a type of routine maintenance that can keep your canine credit score in good shape. The best case scenario is that you use your dog's trained skills very frequently on credit and then reliably reinforce them for their behavior to pay it off in full.

Because sometimes you have to take a *big* behavior out on credit. For example, maybe you need to use that expensive emergency recall because your dog is about to sniff a snake on a hike and you ran out of cookies two miles ago. In that moment, the absolute last thing you want is for your dog to have to run a credit check to see whether you're good for it. You want to have a nice, robust credit score so your dog doesn't even think twice before almost *teleporting* back to your side. And the way you get that behavior is by proving to your dog, over and over again, that even if it looks like you have no reinforcement available, you will always promptly repay your debts.

But Wait, We Never Taught Him "NO!"

My gosh, what an oversight! A whole book on dog training and we somehow completely overlooked how to teach the dog "no!"

You're right—and that wasn't an accident, because "no" is not a behavior.

I promise I'm not just being pointlessly contrary. Stick with me for a second, because this is important. Can you point to a dog no-ing? Can you draw me a picture of what "no" looks like?

If your dog is pulling on the leash, then "no" looks like putting slack in the leash. If your dog is jumping, then "no" looks like standing with four feet on the ground. If your dog is getting in the trash can, then "no" looks like turning their head away from the distraction and not engaging with it.

At the risk of stating the obvious, those are *completely unrelated behaviors*.

Because "no" is not a behavior. It's an absence of behavior.

At best, it's a poorly-taught version of leave it using compulsion rather than reinforcement—and that's when it even works. At worst, it's an emotional outburst from the human which has virtually no effect on the dog's long-term behavior. It will probably just stress everybody out, express the person's frustration or intimidate the dog. It's what you automatically yell when something happens that you didn't expect—which is not the same thing as clear information for your dog.

By this point in the book, we've taught your dog to offer attention, to sit and lie down politely, to move toward you for a hand target, to move away from you to go to mat, to resist temptations in the environment, to reduce pressure on the leash, to greet people calmly, to potty outside and promptly when asked, to stay where they are and to stop staying where they are.

That is a pretty broad spectrum of behaviors. I am willing to bet that if you draw me a picture of what that desired result of "no" looks like in any specific situation, it's going to look an awful lot like a variation on one of those behaviors.

Which means instead of saying "no" when your dog gets in the trash, you can cue "leave it" and get the same result: your dog turning their head away from the distraction and not engaging with it. And because "leave it" is a specific trained cue for a behavior they already know how to do, there's almost no chance that they will choose standing-with-four-feet-on-the-ground ("no" for jumping) or putting-slack-in-the-leash ("no" for leash pulling) instead, because you will be telling them exactly what you would like them to do.

And if you slip up and still default to blurting "no" when frustrated once in a while? Congratulations, you're human like the rest of us. Acknowledge it for what it is (an emotional reaction) and don't rely on it to be more than that (e.g. an educational experience for your dog). Make a note that your dog needs more training on whatever-you-needed-to-say-no-about and work on it in your next practice session.

If there are situations in your dog's life where you are routinely saying "no," ask yourself what behavior you would like to see your dog doing instead. In this instance, what would a picture of "no" look like? Is it close to any of the skills that your dog already knows how to do? If you need your dog to move through space, could you ask for a hand target where you would like them to end up? If you need your dog to turn away from a distraction, could you train this scenario as an extension of your leave it practice? Are any of the behaviors that your dog already knows how to do mutually incompatible with the behavior that you want to prevent? (For example, a dog can't jump and sit at the same time, so if you are trying to prevent jumping, you can level up your dog's sit.)

The more you ask yourself, "What *do* I want in this situation," the less often you will feel the need to lean on "no" as a backup plan, because you can proactively prevent most of those undesirable behaviors from happening by telling your dog what you *do* want them to do instead.

In Conclusion

Solving the Theory Dilemma

In the beginning of this book, I told you about my Theory Dilemma: the struggle between fixing my students' problems today and giving them the big-picture context they need to solve their own problems in the future. The two years I've invested in writing this book are my attempt to solve that dilemma so that every student I teach has access to the "why" behind the "how."

As we part ways at the end of this book, I hope that you have several things.

First, a better-behaved dog.

Second, a solid understanding of how that happened.

Third, a working understanding of how to teach a dog with positive reinforcement so that this book will be the first of many steps on your training journey together. I hope that by the time you reread this book or pass it on to a friend, the skills that were challenging for you on your first read-through are second nature to you by the time you revisit them.

And if you've enjoyed this book, I hope you'll take the time to let me know by leaving an honest review and mentioning which parts were the most helpful for you—that's my positive reinforcement!

About the Author

Natalie Bridger Watson spent most of her childhood with her arms full of either (a) a wide variety of excellent books or (b) a wide variety of excellent pets that she probably smuggled home in secret to forestall her parents' protests, so it should surprise exactly no one that she now writes books, works with animals and lives with her own zoo of high-maintenance herdy dogs.

She shares her life with Haven the deaf Australian shepherd, Indi the Shetland sheepdog, Bright the German shepherd/Belgian malinois mix, Theory the German shepherd and very few humans.

When Bridger is not writing epic fantasy novels, she's probably training a dog. She runs a positive reinforcement dog training business by day, trains her own dogs by night and occasionally travels the east coast of the US to compete with other dog trainers in dog sports on the weekend for a busman's holiday. Her dogs are nationally ranked in their respective sports and Bridger hopes to someday be as accomplished as they are.

In her spare time, Bridger collects craft supplies and miscellaneous new hobbies at an alarming rate and shows no signs of stopping.

Bonus Lectures

Mental Versus Physical Exercise

Most of us have heard by now that a tired dog is a good dog and that a dog with a job is likely to be less obnoxious than a dog who makes his own entertainment.

And in pursuit of this goal, many dog owners diligently exercise their dog for hours per day, trying in vain to find the line where their rocket-fuel-for-breakfast dog suddenly becomes the proverbial tired good dog. Or they teach their dog to bring in the mail and hope that counts as a fulfilling job.

In reality, an *enriched* dog is a good dog, and while that often goes along with tired because of how we exercise our dogs, it is entirely possible to have an enriched dog without creating a canine triathlete with six extracurricular activities.

Enrichment is allowing a dog to express their doggy needs and do the things that fill their cup. Think of it as a sort of canine self-care.

You know how much more grounded and fulfilled you feel when you've had adequate sleep, you've exercised appropriately, you've eaten well, you've stayed hydrated, you've spent time with family and friends, you've spent time on your leisure activities and you've worked toward meaningful goals in your life?

Yeah, okay, I know it's a high bar to juggle *all* of that, but you've done *some* of that recently. (And if not, please do. Call it dog training homework. My gift to you.)

Your dog feels that same type of fulfillment and satisfaction with life when they're able to use mental energy on their dog priorities. Dog priorities often involve physical exercise, but they don't *have* to. I'm a huge fan of mental exercise because I have a house full of high energy dogs and only a limited amount of energy myself, so I work hard to keep their brains occupied.

Moving Beyond the Bowl

One of the easiest ways to incorporate more enrichment in your dog's life is to throw away their food bowl. (Or donate it to your local shelter or rescue to improve another dog's life at the same time as yours.)

We talked a little bit about this in the context of training earlier in the book, but if you've been holding out on me, here's another reason to consider.

Food is a central part of your dog's day and food-seeking behavior is a huge chunk of his natural behavioral repertoire. That means that even the pickiest pup can benefit from receiving their food through training or from puzzle toys rather than eating out of a bowl. If you're able to use their food to engage their brain and their body, you'll have a calmer and more satisfied dog at the end of the day, which means less demand behavior for you to navigate. Think of it as draining their energy battery *and* refilling their emotional cup at the same time.

You can make this elaborate or you can do it the easy way.

On days when I'm not able to use most of my dogs' food in training and I've forgotten to stuff their puzzle toys, I'll scatter their food on the floor so they have to use their nose and eyes to find each piece, which encourages them to exercise the hunt-and-seek part of their mind. It's very low-effort for me, but still drains the dogs' batteries enough that they feel fulfilled. (If you have a multi-dog household or a dog who may guard his food from other dogs or people, scatter-feeding should be done in separate rooms or this may not be an appropriate type of enrichment for your dog. Use good judgment here.)

If I'm able to practice my dogs' training, we'll practice for their dinners. That way, we are trading—they're getting the meals they want to eat (and which I would have fed them anyway) and I'm putting mileage on the training skills I want to improve. It's *astounding* how quickly you can make progress if you practice for your dog's dinner every day, or even just a few days a week. It only takes five or ten minutes of investment from you—much less than that hour-long run around the block in a vain attempt to tire out your teenage husky who could pretty much run the Iditarod single-handedly.

Kong as Babysitter

Another great option to keep on hand is a dog toy called a Kong.

There was a time in my life when I thought Kongs were a stupid, overhyped dog toy. I *regret* those days.

Kongs are magic. I have twelve in my freezer as I write this and I would happily triple that number if I could afford to.

A Kong is a snowman-shaped hollow dog toy made of durable rubber. It's not the only type of puzzle toy on the market, but it's the name brand for a reason.

Some of my clients are already using Kongs when we start working together, which is wonderful—gold star from your dog trainer. But the vast majority of them are stuffing the whole Kong with peanut butter, which is the enrichment equivalent of stuffing a $100 bill into a gumball machine instead of a quarter (and it's also likely to make your dog gassy, phew). You don't need to break out the canine Benjamins for this! While Kongs can be as elaborate as a three-course dinner, they can also be as plain as their regular dinner kibble soaked in a bit of warm water and frozen.

You can stuff a Kong with your dog's regular food dampened with water to create a challenging meal puzzle for your dog to figure out. If you're just stuffing one or two Kongs, put them small-side-down into a spare mug and fill them with kibble. Then pour warm water over them and wait for the kibble to swell—you're aiming for a very-soggy-cereal consistency, which usually takes about half an hour of soaking. The mug keeps the Kong upright so the kibble doesn't float out. Once the kibble has soaked and cooled, remove the Kong from the mug carefully and let the extra water drain out the bottom of the Kong.

For a beginner dog, I serve the Kong soaked like this for a couple of days so they get confident with their toy-excavation skills. You want them to be absolutely certain that they can get the last bite at the bottom of the Kong before you make it harder.

Once the dog is more experienced, you can start mashing the kibble down into the Kong so it's more densely packed. When they're a pro at that, start freezing the Kong after soaking it. This step makes it *much* more time-consuming to empty, which means more enrichment for your dog and more peace and quiet for you!

When they've mastered a basic dampened food Kong, you can try mixing in some larger treats or mushy layers of canned food and freezing it overnight for a pupsicle your dog will take ages to solve.

Kongs give your dog more of a mental challenge than eating out of a bowl and they make a great "babysitter" for times when you need to keep your dog occupied but can't be available. They're also wonderful for situations like keeping your dog calm and out of the way while a repairman is in the house or while you're on a conference call for work.

Ring a Bell to Go Outside

Potty training issues are incredibly frustrating, especially when you're working with a dog who is perfectly happy to potty outside as long as you remember to take them out, but won't ask to go out even if they're bursting at the seams.

In an earlier section, we talked about putting potty on cue and reinforcing for going potty outside, and now we're going to add the last component of that: teaching the dog to *ask* to be let outside for the opportunity to potty.

Hang a small bell near your doorway. If you search for "potty bells," you can buy them all sorts of places including many local pet stores, but you can also use a small set of windchimes if that's easier to source. Choose something that isn't excessively loud (for the dog's benefit) or grating on the ears (for your benefit).

When it's time to go outside, hold a treat behind the bells so your dog has to bump the bell with their nose to get the treat. *Any* amount of noise from the bells is enough—they don't need to stick their head in the bells and clatter them, especially in the beginning.

As soon as your dog touches the bell in any way, ideally with their nose, give them the treat, open the door and take them outside on a leash to go potty. Repeat this every time you take the dog out to go potty.

Note: Please don't pick up your dog's foot and physically paw it through the bells. That's not an efficient way to teach this skill and it creeps most dogs out. Use the treat behind the bells and let the dog move their own body. It's much faster in the long term and it's way less creepy and invasive to your dog.

It's also worth noting that I exclusively use the bells as a way to ask for *potty* walks, not exercise walks. Even if you have a fully fenced doggy paradise, put a leash on the dog when they ring the bell in the beginning.

Put on the leash, walk to the same boring spot in the yard, wait for potty. If they don't potty, go back inside without playing or going anywhere interesting. If you have a fenced yard, you can take the leash off *after* they potty, but not before. You don't want your dog to ring the bell every time they see a squirrel in the neighbor's tree, so potty should be the first thing that happens after ringing the bell for best results.

The second half of the equation is to listen for the bells during your day to day life. If the bell rings, take the dog outside, no matter what you were doing, no matter whether the dog just went outside two minutes ago and you *know* they're empty.

Personally, I give every new dog learning the bells one full week to be an absolute tyrant with the bells. For the first week, I will come running every single time they ring (sometimes muttering unkind words under my breath *as* I run, because I'm only human, but I will come). If they ring the bells during that week, we go outside on a leash for five minutes and we stand in a boring part of the yard. The most interesting thing they can do is pee. They learn that they have the power to summon me at a moment's notice, but the only reinforcer it gives them access to is grass to pee on.

Yes, this takes more work than just opening the door and letting them out, especially if you're used to the luxury of a fenced yard. Trust me, a dog who fully understands the bell system (and doesn't abuse the privilege) is worth it.

After a week, you can start gambling if you want. If you're very sure that your dog does not have to potty and you're willing to risk an accident, start to ignore the most egregious bell-ringing ("you were outside *two minutes ago* and I saw you pee *and* poop and I *know* that your bladder is as dry as the Sahara") while still giving them the benefit of the doubt on anything questionable. Continue to walk them on leash in the yard and keep it fairly boring. It usually takes another week or so before they're consistent with ringing the bells every time they have to potty but not abusing the privilege.

And at any stage of training, the potty bells are never used to go outside to play. Potty bells are used for potty and that's it. The stricter you can be about that in the beginning, the easier it will be in the long term. If you let that be a slippery slope, it will become one.

When your dog is using their bells reliably and responsibly to ask to go outside and you're rarely getting "false alarms," you can start to do the same routine without the leash. You should still accompany your dog outside, wait for potty first, reward, then allow them to play afterward if you'd like. If you start getting false alarms, add more structure back in.

Pretty soon, you will have a dog who alerts you when they need to go potty outside by ringing their potty bells, which you can hear from anywhere in the house.

Why We Don't Say Hi on Leash

Some distractions are both wild and entirely preventable—and in my opinion, best avoided. That category is greetings on a leash, particularly dog/dog greetings with dogs who don't know each other.

Most of my clients look at me like I've shot them when I say this, but I know exactly zero dog trainers (out of hundreds of colleagues) who think it is a good idea to allow strange dogs to meet each other on the average neighborhood walk.

Not one. Not a few. Zero.

The reality is that on leash greetings create so many more problems than they solve. In our efforts to socialize our dogs, we often accidentally teach them that charging up to strange dogs is an appropriate behavior, and it's not. It's the dog equivalent of running up to a stranger on the sidewalk and kissing them. If your dog has even been growled at by a stranger's dog when they were "just being friendly," there is a better than decent chance that your dog was guilty of kissing a stranger on a street.

Dogs are a social species and bless them, they forgive a lot of errors. And there's nothing more heartwarming than dogs who get along and want to play together.

However, play should be off leash, in a safe environment and ideally with familiar dogs with similar play styles (wrestlers with wrestlers, chasers with chasees, and so on). If you build the expectation that your dog will be able to play with any dog they see on their own terms, you're going to create a dog who is so magnetically drawn to other dogs that they will be absolutely miserable to walk with because they will be motivated to haul you toward everything with four legs.

And while people are shocked to hear that I do not recommend letting unfamiliar dogs meet on leash (nor, I reiterate, does literally any competent trainer I have ever met in my entire career), this becomes completely obvious when you translate it to kid behavior.

Think of it this way. You're in the grocery store because you need to buy something. Your kid is with you because they're your kid and they go places with you. But you have adult priorities and you're just here to get a few essentials before you can head home for the night for some well-deserved rest.

If your kid spots another kid in the grocery store, would it be socially appropriate for them to immediately run across the store to "go say hi" to the other kid they don't know? Would you stop your grocery shopping or even steer your cart over to the other family to facilitate that? Would you expect the rest of the grocery store's shoppers to smile with benign indulgence as your kids played tag in the middle of the aisle until one or both of them decided they were ready to move on while you swapped parenting stories with the other parent?

No, because that sounds crazy.

That behavior might be appropriate at a school function, a children's extracurricular lesson or on a playground, but it's absurd in a grocery store, a place where we are socialized to stay in our proverbial lane. We expect even very young kids to be able to distinguish between when they will be able to play with the peers around them and when they're expected to be socially unavailable to strangers.

And if your kid was howling and wailing that they desperately *needed* to go play with the other random stranger across the store, it would never cross your mind that the correct solution was to say, "Well, just this once. You're just *so* friendly!" and let your kid race over to bother a stranger in an attempt to pacify their hysterics. That would be nuts.

Dogs? Yep, same.

The rule in my house is that if the leash is on, the dog does not greet other dogs at all. I also ask my dogs to ignore vastly more people than they get to actually interact with. If I tried to put a number on it, I'd guess that my dogs get to say hi to about 2% of the people they see on any given day and 0% of the dogs they meet on a walk.

And I share my friendly, well-trained dogs with other people as part of my job.

You can turn the wild distraction of people and other dogs into a tame distraction by setting the firm expectation from early on in your dog's life that they simply won't be able to interact with other people or dogs on a leash. Leashed walks are a time for them to engage with the environment or with you.

No, You Can't Pet My Dog

I also don't let most people pet my dogs when we're out walking and I encourage you not to either. Yes, even if your dog is friendly and loves people—sometimes *especially* if your dog is friendly and loves people.

First, I want to set the expectation that dogs are not in public to be interacted with. The US is the only country in the world where pet dogs are seen as almost public property and where dog hysteria has reached the point where asking to play with a complete stranger's dog is not only acceptable but the social norm. People are *offended* when you say that they can't pet your dog, as if they have more right to touch your dog's body than your dog has to exist in the world without being touched.

Second, I want kids to hear an adult tell another adult that they cannot pet their dog who appears friendly. We teach kids to ask before petting, but we often neglect to teach them to listen for and respect the no, and to ask from a distance so they aren't inches from the dog's body before asking whether the dog is okay with kids or not. I want it to be socially normal to decline the request, and I model that behavior.

Third, strangers largely do not care if your dog jumps, which is a problem if you *do* care that your dog jumps and would like them to not do that in the future. (If I had a nickel for every time I've heard, "Oh, I don't mind!" Well, *I* mind and I'm the one who will be living with this dog for the next decade, so you don't get to undo my training by being "nice" to my dog by encouraging them to be impolite to you.)

And fourth, as above, this is a distraction that we create for ourselves and can completely prevent. If we teach our dogs that strangers on walks are not for interacting with, we remove one of the most potent distractions in the environment.

Trail and Sidewalk Manners

So, if I'm so keen on avoiding people and dogs, how do I keep my dogs from accessing those things? And how do I keep well-meaning, too-friendly people from overstepping my boundaries?

Answer: I practice trail and sidewalk manners ahead of time so my dogs know what to do in the case of a social distraction.

If I see a person approaching on a path toward me, I step off the side of the road with my back to the sidewalk (yes, even if this means stepping a few feet into someone's yard) and lure my dog in front of me so that my body is between my dog and the other person's path of travel.

With a novice dog, I pay them continuously the entire time that a person is passing so that the dog's attention is glued to me. And I mean fast enough that they would have to almost spit out the next treat to look at the stranger because I am not even giving them enough space between treats to make the wrong decision. I want it to be overwhelmingly obvious that a stranger approaching is a cue to focus *intensely* on me no matter what that stranger does.

With a more experienced dog, I ask for a sit stay, reward as needed to support that, then go on my way after the person has passed.

I practice this when there are no people as well so the skill is fluent and easy. Since my neighborhood does not have nice sidewalks, I also step off the road for passing cars, because I want my dogs to have plenty of practice getting out of traffic if they hear a car approaching. At this point, my dogs often see the distractions before I do and head to the side of the road to wait for their ignoring-the-thing cookie with almost no effort on my part, which is just how I like it. How civilized! It completely prevents an awful lot of pulling, jumping, barking and socially reinforced behaviors that I don't want to have to undo later.

If this is not an option, or if I am working with a dog who is too excited by people or dogs to wait politely by the side of the trail and who needs an easier starting point, I teach my dogs an emergency U-turn.

To do that, first you'll say, "Fido, let's go!" and then pivot 180 degrees clockwise so you are facing in the opposite direction. Take a few quick steps away and give your dog several treats when they catch up with you in the new direction. "Let's go!" will become the cue to turn around and quickly pay attention to you as you move away from a distraction. And it's always worthwhile to practice this on your regular walks when nothing interesting is happening to make sure the skill is nice and strong. If you see a distraction approaching that you suspect will be too exciting for your dog's experience level, you can say "Let's go!" and preemptively move in a different direction before your dog has a chance to make an error.

In Case of Emergency: It's Okay to Lure Past

Sometimes, though, you just need to get past something and your dog doesn't have the skills to navigate that distraction safely. Sometimes there's a kid on a tricycle between the trail and your car. Sometimes you need to get your just-too-friendly dog through a packed-to-the-brim vet's office without them crawling into another dog's cone of shame to say hello to their new BFF up close and personal.

You have some tricks up your sleeve already to help them through.

If it's a mild distraction and you just need to help a little bit, using a hand target or two can be enough to patch you through a rough spot, such as getting through a doorway if your dog balks at thresholds, moving through a narrow space without knocking stuff off shelves or dodging a particularly gross mud puddle on the trail.

In a more emotionally loaded situation, such as getting an excitable dog through a vet clinic or getting your dog out of the path of a lunging dog on a leash, put a cookie directly on your dog's lips and lure them where you need them to go.

Is it training? No, it's management. It's damage-control and that's fine.

Yes, we want to fade luring quickly when we're using it for training purposes, and yes, someone may make a shitty comment about bribery. But dear god, if you're in a tight spot and one cookie keeps your dog's brain in their skull and helps them make the right decision this time so they can make it more easily next time, just lure past. You're allowed. I hereby give you permission. I would rather see you lure around a distraction that your dog can't handle yet than watch your dog have a meltdown because they were in a situation beyond their current skill level.

Made in the USA
Las Vegas, NV
31 August 2023

76891677R00129